In God's Hands, In God's Time

We are Connected to Heaven

Paul Stefaniak

ISBN: 0692238050
ISBN 13: 9780692238059
Library of Congress Control Number: 2014911154
C.J.Terry Books, Grand Junction, CO
Cover photo credit: Joel M. Stefaniak

To Terry, Chris, and Joel
for their love, support,
and encouragement.

Contents

Introduction

"You are destined to work with us and your soul knows it. Your life is as you planned it... we are just helping you along the path you chose."

I found this quote in one of my meditation journals. It comes from one of my Guardian Angels, who repeatedly insists that I share the experiences I've had on my personal spiritual journey. The book's title is, in fact, my Angels' standard response to my ongoing frustration and the equivalent of a weary parent telling a demanding child "Not yet" or "We'll see." They usually add a *"Dear Paul"* at the end to comfort me and to make me realize that I am truly in contact with Spirit since no living person on this planet refers to me as "Dear Paul."

These chapters describe how my journey has evolved from a few ghostly encounters in thirty-six years while I just "lived my life" to life-altering events that have stimulated my curiosity to pursue years of research, study, after-death communications, and ongoing spiritual contact. I refer to my journey as climbing the rungs on a ladder—as soon as I successfully take one step up, I need another. I need to climb higher and learn more, and the more information I receive, the more I seek. The more I seek, the more that is revealed to me. As you share my journey, you may be reminded of personal experiences that you may have dismissed or even doubted. "No, this can't be real. I must be imagining it." Sound familiar? I was uncertain and skeptical at one time, as well.

Whatever the case, by the final page you will be certain of at least one thing—you have a decision to make. You've climbed the ladder along with me, and now you must decide if you will continue on, or climb back down. Has your curiosity been piqued enough to pursue a journey of your own? Or do you believe that you aren't capable—or deserving of—receiving spiritual communication?

Either way, you are correct. If you make the effort and do the work, you'll be open to Spirit. If you choose not to, Spirit will understand. It's called Free Will. After all, isn't that how you are living your life right now?

Regardless of your choice, you'll be up on the ladder where the next rungs may lead you to your Angels, Guides, and Departed Loved Ones, while the rungs you've already climbed will lead you back to the life you already have.

Not much of a choice, is it?

My mother's passing awakened my spiritual journey. Emily retired from the U.S. Postal Service in 1990. Three weeks later she was diagnosed with multiple myeloma, a cancer that starts in the plasma cells in bone marrow. The cells grow out of control in the bone marrow and form tumors that weaken the bone, causing pain and weakness. Mom's suffering was sadly and mercifully brief. She passed within nine months of her diagnosis. Our relationship was not always close, but the pain and confusion that consumed me was no less real. Why did she have to suffer so? What happened to her after she passed? Why did I feel her absence so deeply?

My confusion gave way to curiosity, and through prayer, meditation, and research, I felt my pain was lessening, and I began my lessons in earnest. I was raised Catholic and had twelve years of religious education to fall back on, but I needed some personal answers. I read somewhere that a religious person adheres to the doctrine of his church, while a spiritual person follows the guidance of his soul. That resonated within me.

In the thirteen months before my mother's death, I had two puzzling experiences of my own. In the first, I saw a vision of a brown car suspended thirty feet in the air over a meadow, and moments later I experienced a second vision of the same brown car farther up the road, and this led to the rescue of a family of six when I recklessly took action, caused thirty fender benders, and led seventy-five travelers down a snowy hillside to the scene of the accident.

The second time, I was drowning and spared from death by a miracle when, as I blacked out, I asked God a simple question.

Two life-altering events followed by my mother's fatal illness and deathbed revelations within thirteen months made me very curious. I started reading books on death, near-death experiences, spirituality, past-life regressions, and the like. I practiced meditation and had success within a few weeks. When I became frightened during a past-life regression, I utilized the services of a hypnotherapist. I learned quickly, and was soon able to make contact with the Other Side. I met Angels, Spirit Guides, Departed Loved Ones—also known as Spirit—and witnessed myself in past lives. The more I experienced, the more I wanted to learn. I became passionate about spirituality.

This book covers my experiences over a twenty-three-year period. Mine are different from those of people who have visited Heaven during near-death experiences and share how it changed their lives. I didn't have the typical near-death experience where my heart stopped, and I visited Heaven—an experience that skeptics could later claim that my struggling brain came up with fantasies of the Other Side. In my two life-savings events, I was on the brink of death—mere seconds away—and spoke to God and my Angels, and two miracles saved my life.

My journey consists of ongoing visits to the Other Side escorted by my Angels and Guides, as well as their communications I refer to as little "hellos" that let me know they are in my life, that I am still on path, and that my destiny has yet to be realized.

Spirit repeatedly has suggested that I document my experiences, most recently during my recovery from a severe injury suffered when I attempted to investigate one of the miracles. While my favorite authors supplement their teachings with their clients' stories, I have been encouraged by Spirit to share my own.

Sixteen years ago two authors of books on after-death communications and on contacts with Angels and Spirits suggested I write one of my own after I shared a few of my experiences with them. It has taken me this long—along with a lot of prodding from Spirit—to get around to it. I've always felt that my experiences are too personal and humbling to share, but there is nothing like lying on your back for two months to get the process started.

From my meditation notes, these thoughts from Spirit:

"Share yourself with others now. You will be thrilled once you let yourself go. Trust us. Write your experiences down. Yes, that is part of your journey. Write it now. The important thing is to start. Don't doubt your ability. Look to writing it as a How-to Book: Here's what happened

to me; how about you? Begin writing and get in touch with your sensibility. Do not fear it. Do not care about what anyone else says or thinks. This is your truth and your destiny, is it not?"

What I've experienced is real, and I have not embellished in any way in writing this book. I have developed ongoing relationships with two Guardian Angels and my Spirit Guide, and I have met dozens more along the way. I have visited with departed family members and friends who have shared their messages of love and support to let me know that they have been aware of what was happening in my life and with my family. These Departed Loved Ones are truly alive, well, and happy in Heaven, enjoying their reunion with family and friends, education, entertainment, and spiritual growth.

My intention is to share this information, and my hope is that you'll rethink the "coincidences" in your life and wonder if they were actually Spirit making their presence known so you can welcome them into your life. If inspired, perhaps you'll focus on your spirituality. I wasn't born with psychic abilities, nor do I claim to have them, but by being open, learning, and trying to make contact with the Other Side, I have had years of experiences—some miraculous and lifesaving—along with hundreds of contacts from Spirit that made me realize that my Angels, Guides, and Departed Loved Ones are always in my life. Simply put: I see what they want me to see and hear what they want me to hear.

You can do so, as well, but you have to try, one step at a time, one rung at a time. That's how you'll get there, led by Spirit.

Please remember that I was searching for answers to questions I had about life, death, and the unexplained events I witnessed. Throughout this book, I'll share my messages from Spirit in *italics,* taken from my meditation journals. Perhaps you'll respond to Spirit's guidance with a sense of calm or peacefulness, a sudden chill or goose bumps, or with your eyes welling with tears. When this happens to me, I believe it's because their message has been recognized by my soul.

"Do not be fearful. Be humble and feel blessed. You are always in God's Hands."

PART ONE:

My Journey

one

The Little Boy in the Attic

The first two chapters of this book cover my first paranormal experiences with ghosts, primarily to demonstrate that I did not have contact with Spirit until I was thirty-six. I was not someone who had psychic experiences throughout my childhood nor did I show any interest in the subject. I was just living my life like everyone else until Spirit made itself known to me.

I got my own bedroom when I was a three-year-old, and it was one of three empty rooms in the attic. It had a bare wooden floor, walls, a peaked roof, and a big-boy bed. My father was the youngest of thirteen children and the last to marry, so he lived at home and took care of his elderly parents. Every night I'd go upstairs and was tucked in by my parents in an otherwise empty room. I was not especially happy there, since my parents, grandparents, and older sister all had bedrooms downstairs. I was upstairs all alone.

Well, I wasn't exactly alone. There was a young man up there with me—a ghost or maybe a Spirit Guide. I've suspected both and never determined which one. I'd lie in bed in the middle room and look towards the back room with the curtain-free window that overlooked the backyard. With thirteen children in the family, I'm sure that all three rooms had teemed with activity for decades, but in 1956 they were completely empty except for my bed. My grandparents didn't have a lot of junk to fill the attic—just a three-year-old and his ghost.

I'd lie in bed and see a young man in the doorway across the room. His arms were folded across his chest, and he'd casually lean against the frame, backlit by moonlight coming through the window. He never said anything. He'd just stand and look at me. I'd scream, "Mom! Dad!" and they'd run up the stairs and ask me what was wrong. I'd hide under the covers and point to the now-empty doorway. I cried that there was a man standing there looking at me. At three, I didn't know what a ghost was, but a young man I could figure out. They never saw the ghost—or believed me. They just told me I was imagining it.

"Then you sleep up here, and I'll sleep downstairs." I may have only been three, but I wasn't stupid. They never fell for it. I stayed up there for almost three years and hated every night of it. After being tucked in, I'd shut my eyes tight and fall asleep, and then I'd wake up and run downstairs every morning. The ghost never came close or spoke to me; he merely stood twenty feet away and stared.

My bed had old feather pillows with little holes in the ends, and I used to pull feathers out and throw them on the bare floor in an act of rebellion. Mom would ask where these piles of feathers came from, and I'd feign ignorance. If she wouldn't acknowledge the ghost, I wouldn't cop to the feathers.

When I was twelve, I overheard my uncle talking about one of his brothers who was a boxer. He was sparring up in the attic with my grandfather, was hit, and died when his head struck the floor. Perhaps he was the young man I saw.

Just a note: remember the feathers because one will initiate a miracle in April 2000. This is how I began my spiritual adventures, as a frightened little boy who insisted that a young man only he could see was a reality. And my adventures continue to this day, only I've lost my fear.

But that wasn't my only experience with a ghost.

two

Ghosts

I believe that ghosts are spirits who refuse to travel to the Other Side and remain earthbound either because they don't believe—or accept— that they are dead, or they fear what lies ahead for them. Fifteen years passed between my ghostly encounters, and I now realize that I was sensitive to their presence.

I served in the USAF in England and spent one Christmas Eve with friends who told me that they believed their centuries-old stone house was haunted by an eighty-year-old woman. Decades earlier she had fallen down the narrow wooden steps that led into the dungeon-like basement and had broken her neck and died. Fa-la-la-la-la, thanks for the Christmas Cheer.

This ghost liked to play with the heaters in their home. In 1974, heating was very expensive, and typically only the living room and bedrooms were heated by the type of heaters used for camping. Their ghost often would turn up the controls on the heaters to the maximum setting and create a contained roaring blaze. She also liked to play with the light switches in the home.

As they told me stories of her haunting, I sat across the living room on a sofa with a view through the kitchen to the bathroom and the door to the basement. Suddenly the bathroom lights began to turn on and off rapidly, but I was the only one who could see this. Maybe the ghost knew she was the topic of conversation, and she wanted to make her presence known to us—or just to me.

Ghost or not, I really needed to use the loo. Scared out of my mind, I gathered enough courage and hurried over. The light stopped its dance, and I used the facility with my eyes tightly shut. I then safely made it back to the living room without seeing their Old Lady Ghost.

But I never went back to that house.

Four months later I rented a house an hour from London in a village that was once the site of a Roman camp. The house was actually one-third of a large Georgian home with farmland behind it. My third had a walled garden bordered with rose bushes and a side door into the living room. There was a back door that led to two entry halls, a bathroom, a kitchen, and a living room downstairs. An enclosed staircase from the kitchen led to two bedrooms upstairs. It was bright, cute, and perfect.

The owners were a young couple, a policeman and his pregnant wife. They had just lost their five-year-old son to a heart ailment, couldn't bear to live there any longer, and had put their home up for rent. We first met at the wife's parents' home, which was nearby. I noticed a framed photo of a young boy—the kind where the eyes follow as you move across the room. I jokingly remarked: "He has the look of the Devil in him," an English saying that meant he looked like a fun, spirited child.

After an uncomfortable pause, I was told that the boy had recently passed. I felt foolish, but I was absolutely right. He was a spirited child.

On our first night in the house, as my then-wife and I went to bed, we heard loud noises coming from the kitchen below. Our bedroom was at the top of the staircase that led down to the kitchen. It was obvious that the kitchen table and chairs were being dragged across the lino-leum floor. I knew it for a fact because I had moved them myself from the center of the kitchen and against a wall with a small door secured by a deadbolt lock and leading to a storage area under the stairs. If you can visualize Harry Potter's bedroom at his uncle's house, you've nailed it.

When we toured the home, the mother said that her son had kept all of his toys in that storage closet, and now I had blocked the access to it with the table and chairs. We could hear the deadbolt lock being pulled back and the door flung open hard enough to slam against the wall. We thought burglars were downstairs and decided to stay put. We had only a little television and an expensive stereo system in the living room—a small price compared to our safety.

It soon became quiet downstairs, and we eventually fell asleep. The next morning I went to the kitchen and found the table and four chairs scattered haphazardly across the kitchen. The little storage door in the wall was wide open. I quickly put everything back in place, and then I checked the living room. The television and stereo were still there. That's odd. Who would break in and not steal anything? Oh, that's right, a ghost!

Each night at bedtime, I'd close the bedroom door, climb into bed, and settle in under the covers. Within a minute, the door handle would turn and the door slowly open about a foot. Then a young boy's screams of "Daddy" would follow from the second bedroom—the little boy's room.

It happened every night—the opened door, a few loud cries, and then silence. I avoided that room entirely. If you had a sick child, wouldn't you leave your bedroom door open a bit so you could hear him? And it's easy to imagine a sick child crying out for his Daddy, isn't it?

Our Boy Ghost liked to throw shoes down the stairs and shred art posters from the Royal Gallery in London. I'd be in bed and could hear this happening on the other side of the bedroom door as I pulled the covers over my head. I'd eventually fall asleep and clean up the mess in the morning.

My Boy Ghost sometimes would turn on the stereo at full blast at three a.m. After running downstairs a few times to turn it off, I eventually figured out to just unplug it. This may seem hard to believe, but the neighbors never spoke to us about this, although I did get used to their dirty looks.

I'd watch television in the living room, and Boy Ghost would play with the lights and the television. He would flash the lights on and off, change channels or turn the TV off. The old-fashioned English light switches and televisions had finger-like protrusions—push one in and another would pop out. I could see them being manipulated, although I never saw our Boy Ghost do the deed.

He also liked to throw my collection of antique pewter mugs and autographed softballs from the base team where they were displayed on the mantel above the fireplace. I would sit on the sofa and could see the items move slowly just before they hurtled towards me. At times the softballs would drop and harmlessly bounce on the floor, as they would if a young child tried to throw a ball, but it slipped out of his hand and fell behind him.

This happened frequently, especially when I was home alone. I'm really good with kids, and once I realized the ghost was a lost little boy, I began to talk to him. I'd tell him "OK, this is fun, but I've had enough," and eventually his bad behavior would stop.

If you were in a twelve-by-twelve-foot room with flying mugs and balls, dancing lights, and a television with a mind of its own, what would you do? Tell your friends and have them think you were crazy and never visit? Tell the nice owners and upset the six-month pregnant wife? I do regret not asking the grumpy farmer next door for the boy's name so I could properly address him. I wonder how I would have started that conversation.

Excuse me, but could you tell me the name of the boy that used to live here? He doesn't seem to know that he's dead, and he's the reason the stereo comes on in the middle of the night.

Oh, I should have gone with that. Hindsight, right?

Our friends who lived with the Old Lady Ghost came with their two young boys for dinner one evening. The wives and children sat in the living room and kept the door to the kitchen closed. The husband, an MP I'll call "Billy," sat at the kitchen table, which we had moved back to the center of the room to avoid nightly screeching from moving furniture. I stood at the stove and prepared dinner as we enjoyed our beers and chatted.

A movement across the kitchen suddenly caught my eye. The message board that we used because we worked different schedules hung on the back of the kitchen door, and this began to move. The message board slowly rose and separated from the door, cleared the hook, and crashed to the floor. Not wanting to come clean about our ghost, I casually walked over, picked it up, and placed it back on the hook, never once stopping my casual chatter. Billy looked confused but said nothing.

Boy Ghost wanted to keep playing. Back at the stove, I glanced at the door and spied the board once again rising ever so slowly until it cleared the hook and flew three feet from the door to scare Billy, a military cop. I hurried over to replace it, babbled some distracting nonsense, and hoped I wouldn't have to explain.

I believe a five-year-old would have to reach up and lift the bottom of the grease board carefully so that it angled up and then cleared the hook. That's why it happened so slowly.

Well, the message board moved "by itself" a third time, flying six feet across the kitchen. I replaced it and continued to chat nervously, as Billy stared in silence. Then it flew a fourth time across the kitchen striking the living room door. BAM! Our wives and the two boys ran in to see what was going on.

Billy jumped up and screamed, "You've got a ghost!"

"Yeah, but just a little one," I confessed as I hurried over and picked the message board off the floor.

Boy Ghost must have just wanted to play with Billy's two young sons, and the closed door to the living room was an obstacle. The rest of the evening was unremarkable, but Billy and his family never visited us again. You'd think since they had their own ghost they'd be more open and receptive, but I guess a message board whizzing past your head can lead to appararition-intolerance.

The final straw came on a Saturday afternoon when I was watching a Bette Davis movie on TV and waiting for my then-wife to return from work. I heard the outside door open and close, followed by the sound of footsteps through a long, narrow hallway, a greenhouse-like add-on to this old home. Then the door that led into a small hall inside the house opened and closed, followed by more footsteps. The kitchen door opened and closed, and footsteps crossed the floor and headed my way. They finally stopped two feet behind my head, and I wondered why she didn't say anything. I realized that she must be trying to scare me, and then suddenly the glass knob on the door that led to the rose garden rattled violently.

I'm done with this, I thought. I spun around and shouted *"BOO!"* with all my might, only to see that she wasn't standing there—no one was. But the air in that little space was filled with a great sense of fear, both my Boy Ghost's and mine. I think I scared him as much as he scared me, but I grabbed a blanket and covered my head until my then-wife came home. I don't know what he did, but now that he had snuck up on me after manipulating three doors, plus hearing footsteps across three rooms, I was afraid he'd give me a heart attack. Luckily, we were scheduled to deploy back to the States and were able to move back onto the base three days later. I spent three months with a very active ghost and had no doubt that ghosts really exist. Imagine having an invisible five-year-old boy running around in your home and screaming *"Daddy!"* every night. How long would you have lasted?

I still feel guilty that I was not knowledgeable enough to help this young spirit. I never told his parents. How do you tell a mother and father their young son doesn't know he's dead and is still in their home? We left, and they rented the house to some people we worked with—and whom we didn't tell. I located the house on Google Earth a few years ago, contacted the local newspaper, and asked if there were any reports of ghosts in that home. I never got a reply. I certainly hope that little boy made it to the Other Side, and one day I'll know for sure.

Have you had any ghostly experiences in your life that you have simply dismissed, thinking that it couldn't possibly be real? Do you know of any family or friends who have? Be quiet, still your mind, and then ask what do I need to remember about any ghostly encounters in my life? Write down anything that comes to mind.

three

Romantic Soul Mate

⌒

I want to introduce you to my wonderful wife, Terry. She has been supportive, nurturing, and involved in some of the larger events of my journey.

One night, as I finished writing for the day, I realized that I had forgotten to write the story of how I met her. The next morning, as I flipped through psychic medium and author Kim O'Neill's book *Discover Your Spiritual Destiny,* I checked for my favorite passages, underlined as usual. I saw a paragraph and one specific sentence applicable to my story. And the kicker is – I grabbed the wrong book! That must have been Spirit's way of telling me I am correct to include this section.

In July, 1987, my two sons were in Oregon visiting their mother, and I was invited to watch a coed softball game in a Denver Hospital League. I played softball in Evergreen, a wonderful little town in the mountains with Barry, and he played on the coed team as well. He said that I should come and meet nice people and drink some beer. I can do that.

I parked along the curb next to the softball field and walked across the grass towards the third base side where Barry's team gathered minutes before the game began. As I walked across the batter's area, I stepped on home plate, looked up, and saw Terry as she stood in her sweatpants and red t-shirt. One look and I said out loud to no one that "I'm going to marry that woman."

I've told that story ever since. At first glance my soul recognized hers, and it was love at first sight. For me, at least. I was asked to play on the team and readily accepted. They were, in fact, nice people and had plenty of cold beer – a match made in Heaven. Terry was dating someone and not interested in "some miscellaneous man." By the end of September she came around. She tracked me down at a softball game and said that she couldn't get me out of her mind. She was having nightmares about me and Barry—I'm not taking all of the blame—and she wanted to talk. I asked her to dinner the next night, along with Chris and Joel, who were then seven and six. We all got along wonderfully, began dating, moved in together nine months later, and were married in another twelve months. It has been twenty-six years since I said, *"I'm going to marry that woman."* Hey, when I'm right, I'm right.

Back to Kim's book—she writes that when romantic soul mates are reunited, it is commonplace for one or both parties to immediately recognize the other and say to themselves, "I'm going to marry this person." This sudden awareness is caused by information coming from his/her own soul.

Only I didn't say it to myself. I said it out loud in front of at least thirty players and fans. I've always said that my soul recognized Terry's, and today—even though I selected the wrong book—I opened it to the page and paragraph that affirmed my belief.

Is that coincidence or synchronicity? A coincidence is when things happen at the same time by accident, but seems to have some connection. Synchronicity means that our world is perfectly ordered and planned, and everything is a meaningful coincidence, or perhaps a little "hello" from the Other Side to let us know that we are on path and our life is in order.

My Angels and Guides often come through in my meditations with messages of love, admiration, thanks, and encouragement for me to give to Terry. She is a very gifted soul on her own spiritual journey, and her wisdom and grace are often recognized and appreciated on the Other Side.

Do you have a romantic soul mate in your life? If so, recall how you were brought together. If not, don't give up. It's worth the time and effort.

four

Clairvoyance and the Brown Car

⟶

Clairvoyance means "clear seeing." Spirit puts before us a vision that we are able to see inside our mind's eye or outside of ourselves. The following story relates the first big spiritual event of my journey and my first wake-up call.

On Thanksgiving weekend in 1989, our family spent a few days in Durango, Colorado. We visited Mesa Verde to view the cliff dwelling ruins, and I thought how horrible it must have been to live in such isolation. We left Sunday morning for the trip back to Denver and soon drove right into a blizzard. Terry was behind the wheel—one of the handful of times in our years together because I'm such a terrible passenger.

Through the blinding snow, we drove ten miles an hour for two hours by following the taillights of other cars when we were lucky enough to. All I remember seeing for two hours was the park sign at Wolf Creek Pass, where three teenagers were standing outside of their car and probably deciding not to continue on like we were.

We finally escaped the storm, and it stopped snowing as we passed a utility station on the shoulder of the winding two-lane road. I was emotionally drained and relieved when I saw trees and a meadow straight ahead of us, but then I saw something that I just couldn't believe.

In the meadow a brown car hung in the air, about thirty feet above the ground. Its front end pointed down towards the snow. I stared at it for a few seconds and then covered my eyes with both hands as the road curved north and left, the eerie sight behind me.

I rubbed my eyes hard for about ten seconds, and then looked out the windshield. To my horror, the same brown car was up ahead about two hundred feet, still hanging upside down but lower—maybe twenty feet above the shoulder to our left. I stared in disbelief, and then it suddenly dropped straight down and disappeared into the snow-covered shoulder of the two-lane road. It didn't slide down the hillside; it appeared to enter the snow and disappeared as it dropped in a perfectly straight line.

I grabbed the steering wheel and screamed for Terry to stop the car. I tugged and pulled on the steering wheel as Terry fought to maintain the car's balance on the ice-covered road. I screamed that a car just crashed, and we needed to stop and help. She shouted that she didn't see any approaching car or a car crash, but I insisted and pulled hard on the wheel.

There were no cars in front of us or any approaching from the north. I spotted a large shoulder ahead on the right and shouted at Terry to pull into it. She did, confused, since I'm not the type of person who grabs steering wheels on icy roads or screams about hovering brown cars.

At least I wasn't until that moment.

I got out of the car and ran into the road. A light blue sedan approached slowly. I stepped in front of it with my hands extended and yelled for it to stop. Since the road was a sheet of ice, the sedan was probably doing ten to fifteen miles per hour—which was good because the grill of the car struck my legs, and I fell forward onto its hood as it finally stopped. A couple in their seventies were in the car, and the man rolled down his side window and calmly asked, "What's going on, young fella?"

"A car crashed back there. Can you sit here and block traffic so I can get some help?"

"Sure, be glad to," he said with a smile. He had been behind us for two long, desperate hours, and sitting there, rather than driving into the town of South Fork, was admirable.

I hurried around his car and headed back towards the spot where I saw the brown car drop. "Hurried" is wrong. I slipped, slid, and struggled with my balance every step in my running shoes and track-suit. Oblivious to any vehicles that might be coming from behind me; I hurried down the center of the road and began to notice a long line of cars to my left that had all suddenly stopped hard. Apparently I had caused about thirty fender benders. Drivers rolled down their window and asked what was going on.

"A car crashed, and I need help!" I yelled repeatedly as, pushing forward, I passed more and more cars. I said out loud, "Please God, don't let me see any dead kids," and a second later, I heard a little girl's screams coming from across the road and down the hill to my right. I raced across and didn't bother to look back to see if any vehicles were about to run me down.

When I reached the shoulder of the road, I took off my red Buffalo Bills' cap and threw it down on the snow as a marker in case I needed to be rescued. The snow was two feet deep and the hillside too steep to descend, so I traversed it, going down and to my left towards the woods and the little girl's repeated cries.

I looked down as I angled through the deep snow, then glanced to my right and saw it—the brown car, almost a hundred feet away. It was upside-down and on its hood. All four tires were spinning, and steam rose from the bottom of the front end. The side facing me was com-pacted, and the roof rested on the passenger door. The windows had all been blown out.

I made my way to the bottom of the slope where a fallen tree blocked my path to the car. I'm six-foot-five, and the tree's trunk came up to my armpits. I couldn't see either end of it, and I wondered what to do next when suddenly a man in his late-twenties rose up from the far side of the wreckage and stared at me in disbelief. He hurried around the back of the car with a three-year-old blond girl and a small brown suitcase in his arms. He stopped on the other side of the trunk and handed me the crying child and the suitcase. Then with a look of amazement on his face, he asked, "Where did all you people come from?"

"What people?" In my haste to run to only-God-knew-where I had looked only straight ahead and tried to stay upright.

I turned around and saw the hillside lined with people who stood in my footprints in the deep snow. There must have been seventy-five of them waiting in line, like a bucket brigade.

I never saw one person get out of a car or follow me down the hillside.

I helped four children, all under five years old, over the tree trunk, plus their mom, dad, and a couple of suitcases. Their dog, a yellow lab, made his own way around the tree trunk. The kids were crying, and the tiny mom was in shock and silent. The dad was thrilled. We were the last ones back up the hill to the road, and he told me it was a miracle, and that we saved their lives. I knew we didn't save their lives because we all got down the hillside so they could have made it up to the road, walked back to town, or waited for a passing car.

Surviving that crash was the miracle. Seeing seventy-five people lined up and waiting to help was the miracle. I didn't say anything and just smiled.

When we made it back to the road, it was as if a party had broken out. The rescuers were very excited to help this young family who were in Arkansas for Thanksgiving and headed back to California. They were probably driving too fast on the icy road, flew off, and bounced repeatedly down the hill, until their now-destroyed brown car came to a stop.

Some rescuers stared at me, and I knew what they were thinking. They wondered how I knew the car was there. If they didn't see a car go off the road, how did I, since we were all bunched together on a straight section of the roadway? The sky was gray, but visibility was good for about two hundred feet.

The people who had remained in their cars swore at me for their delay. It seemed surreal. Those who helped were so excited and happy, while the ones that remained in their cars were very angry. Perhaps they didn't notice the crying young children passed up the hill by dozens of caring strangers. Or maybe they resented being trapped in their cars ten more minutes after two hours in a blizzard. After all, thirty cars or so were now stuck together because of me.

I picked up my Bills' cap, the one that dozens of people passed as they raced down a snowy hillside because they saw a crazed man running and yelling about a car crash, and they wanted to help. They *chose* to help, not sit in their cars and swear.

Someone said that there was a convenience store and gas station one mile up the road, and we all agreed to meet there. We divided the family into various cars. We took the mom, one of the daughters, and the dog in our car. The mom didn't say a word. She was surely in shock. She had tiny cuts on her hands from the broken windows, and I gave her my handkerchief to stop the minimal bleeding.

I thanked the older couple who had blocked the other cars and had explained what happened. They simply smiled and drove away, freeing the trapped cars at last.

We were the last car to arrive at the convenience store, and it seemed like we were late to the party. Restrooms, food, coffee, and hot chocolate were in great demand, and the place was packed with happy, celebrating people. The overwhelmed clerk was on the phone with the police when I approached. They wanted to know if there were injuries, and if an ambulance was needed. I told her "no", and that only a box of Band-Aids were necessary, but tell the police to get over here to help the family.

My family got some hot chocolate and used the restrooms before we made our way back to the car. The dad thanked me profusely, thrilled that his young family survived this ordeal. A middle-aged couple told me that they went to a motel and got the family a couple of rooms, but the way the husband looked deep into my eyes, I sensed he wondered how I knew about the crash and was dying to ask me.

We never heard anything about the crash or the family afterwards. I checked both Denver newspapers for the next few days for any mention, but I couldn't find anything. I should have called the police but never thought of it.

I was probably in shock myself after having my first adult clairvoyant experience, thirty years after I last saw the ghost in the attic. I saw two visions of a brown car suspended in the air, grabbed the steering wheel on an icy road to force my wife to stop the car, let another car hit my legs, and then asked its driver to block thirty cars filled with people that had just endured a two-hour blizzard. Finally, I ran down the middle of the road like a madman and asked for help with a car crash that I never saw.

That doesn't sound like me at all, but on that Sunday morning I believe I was asked by Spirit to help, and I did.

I believe the first vision of the brown car hanging in the air was shown to get my attention, and the second vision gave me the car's location and inspired me to take action. I've always wondered if the older couple in the second car were Angels, sent to guarantee that the other cars stopped so that the willing occupants would give aid.

I believe that the family had this accident to prevent an even greater one with possible deaths had they driven into the mountain blizzard the rest of us had just escaped.

I believe that Divine Intervention caused their car to slide off the road and tumble down the snowy hillside. Their car was destroyed, but the family of six and their dog escaped with just tiny cuts. After seeing the wreckage of their car, I believe it certainly looked like a miracle.

Divine Intervention prevented this family from multiple serious injuries or even deaths.

Perhaps Divine Intervention allowed this accident to take place, or even caused it.

Remember those words, because that is exactly what happened to me twenty-two years later.

five

The Miracle in the River

*"Know that we are always with you
to help you achieve your destiny."*

Webster's Dictionary defines Miracle as "a surprising and welcome event that is not explicable by natural or scientific laws and is therefore considered to be the work of a Divine Agency." We had a family near-death experience, and my life was spared by God's Miracle when I asked Him a simple question with my final conscious thought. This was the second major event that started me on my spiritual journey.

Seven months after our Brown Car Experience we spent Father's Day weekend in Steamboat Springs, the beautiful ski resort town northwest of Denver. Terry found us a very nice condo rental, and on Saturday morning we decided to take a relaxing inner-tube trip down the Yampa River. Actually, Terry, Chris, and Joel decided, and I went along with it.

We went to a sporting goods store to rent four inner tubes for ten dollars. As I handed the sales clerk the money, another employee walked quickly past and said, "Watch out for the holes in the river."

What? Did I hear that right? But he was gone in an instant, and before I could ask the sales clerk what he meant, I was being given directions and handed four rubbery doughnuts.

We drove out of town to a small parking lot and a place that had easy access to the water. Chris and Joel were ten and nine years old, respectively, and very excited. I was almost thirty-seven and scared to death. I can't swim a stroke—or even hold my breath underwater—and I have been afraid of water since a near-drowning at the age of five.

I remember standing in two inches of water at the shore and having a panic attack. The boys laughed and said, "Dad's scared," as they climbed into their tubes and pushed out into the river. Terry could see that I was not a happy camper, but we were doing this for the boys, and I couldn't back out and disappoint them. We had gone to a rodeo the night before where they had run around the arena and chased a sheep with dozens of other kids. This was another fun, family thing to do on our special weekend, so I had better overcome my anxiety and get with the program because that's what good Dads do.

I was terrified, and I knew it. What was my problem with floating down a peaceful river on a beautiful morning, anyway? What could possibly go wrong? Our instructions were to take the right fork when we reached the island. Kayakers took the fork to the left because it had more rapids. OK, I got it—right is good, and left is bad. How hard could that be?

As we approached the island, Terry spotted the two forks and pointed out a group of about ten kayakers up ahead. They all wore brightly colored outfits with matching helmets and paddled what looked like brand new kayaks. Oh, one more thing, they all paddled into the right fork.

Right is good, left is bad.

Inner tubers go right, and kayakers take the left fork with the bigger rapids. That's what the sales clerk said. Yeah, but I also remembered the short guy who breezed past and told me to watch out for the holes in the river.

Terry needed a decision as we neared the two forks, and I thought that I must have gotten it wrong. Here was a group of kayakers with their expensive equipment and flashy outfits, and they were maneuvering into the right fork so they must be right. We had ten dollars of rented rubber, shorts and T-shirts, so I must be wrong.

"We go to the left." In seconds our tiny flotilla hit the rapids that weren't supposed to be there. Well, they were, but once I convinced myself otherwise, they should have moved over to the right fork. The rapids weren't awful, but more than we anticipated, enough whitewater to get my heart racing.

We got tossed around a bit. Terry, Chris, and Joel loved it. I held onto the sides for dear life, even though I'd estimate that the water that day was no more than three feet at its deepest. My knee was "scoped" two weeks earlier, and despite my futile efforts at protecting it, the inner tube kept turning and twisting in the rapids so that my healing knee struck every available boulder.

And then the trouble began. My inner tube exploded after it struck a rock and was followed by Joel's. We stood in the water, and I commandeered Chris's tube. He sat on Terry's lap, and Joel and I doubled up on the other one.

We were out of the rapids and floating gently again, and I was upset with myself for thinking the kayakers were right and that I chose the wrong fork.

We soon hit another stretch of rapids, and as Joel and I bounced through them, our inner tube struck a large rock. We went airborne—six or seven feet—and rocketed up and to the left towards the concrete wall of an overpass. I grabbed Joel around his waist with my right forearm and leaned down and to the right - twisting so our feet wouldn't hit the wall head-on.

We struck the wall, our inner tube burst, and we were thrown backwards down into the water.

Into a hole in the river!

Disoriented, I sank down to the bottom. I was in a hole, or a pit, in the riverbed. I was in a panic and taking in water through my nose and mouth. I couldn't feel any sides of the hole, and when my feet touched the bottom, I tried to spring back up. I didn't see Joel anywhere, and so I assumed he missed the hole and was safe with Terry and Chris. I can say that now, but then I was probably fretting that I was drowning and needed to get out of there immediately.

I saw the surface of the water a few feet above my outstretched right arm. I struggled with all my might to spring up, but I would fall back down until my feet hit the bottom and I'd try to spring up once again. You get very focused when you know that you will drown if your hand doesn't break the surface. I'd spring up, and then sink back down, over and over. I continued to swallow river water and screamed for help. I felt the pain in my chest as my lungs filled with water, and I knew that I was slowing down and getting father away from breaking the surface with each attempt.

"I'm going to die. I'm going to die right here in front of my wife and sons because I went tubing when I didn't want to." I was furious at myself for being in this horrific situation. "What a stupid way to die. What a stupid, wasted life, ending like this."

I looked up to my left and saw the sun high in the clear blue sky. Its rays filtered through the water. It was beautiful, and a sense of peace and calm overtook me.

I thought how strange it was that at the moment I realized I was about to die, I stopped to notice the beauty of the sun's rays coming towards me through the water. I sprang up, exhausted, and talked to the sun as if it were God. I asked for His help. I asked for my right hand to break the surface so Terry could see it and rescue me. I asked to live for my family so that I could raise my sons, and I asked that they not have to experience this terrible, fatal accident.

Despite my desperate efforts and pleas, I never broke the surface and drifted down for what I knew would be the last time. It seemed like I moved in slow motion. I looked up at the beautiful sun through the watery rays and asked, "God, is that all You wanted from me?"

Everything went black, and I knew my life was over as I sunk deeper into the darkness, silence, and nothingness. I have no idea how long this may have lasted, probably seconds, but here is how my story differs from others who have had near-death experiences: I didn't go to Heaven. I didn't see any Pearly Gates or brilliant white lights. There were no Beings of Light or Angels there to greet me. No Departed Loved Ones, either. I didn't see any indescribable colors or beautiful landscapes, nor did I hear any Choir of Angels or meet St. Peter.

Just the blackness. Just the silence. Just the nothingness.

The next thing I knew, my eyes opened, and I was on my hands and knees, and violently discharging river water—as if I were an open fire hydrant. I was on the very tip of the small island, upstream from the small rapids where Joel and I had gone airborne.

Ten feet to my left were two kayakers, a man and a woman. She screamed, "Where did he come from? He wasn't here a second ago!" Here I was, only ten feet away, when I apparently materialized out of thin air before them—and they just kept going. They didn't stop to help or say anything. They screamed and left me there.

Stunned, I watched over my left shoulder as they hurried away. Their screams alerted my family as they searched in eighteen inches of water. How could someone six-foot-five and two-hundred-and-forty pounds disappear in eighteen inches of water?

Terry, Chris, and Joel ran over and joined me on the island. They waited until I gathered my strength to move on. We crossed the river, climbed the slope, and walked in silence until we reached the main road and caught the trolley back to our car. We returned to the condo, and I spent the next twenty hours in our bedroom in a fetal position where, disgusted by the taste and smell of the river water, I relived the experience again and again.

And we never mentioned the incident for eleven years. Not a single word to anyone or among ourselves.

Eleven years later we invited a friend over for dinner, and she related stories of Angels intervening in people's lives in times of need. I remember vividly that Terry and I exchanged knowing looks as she spoke, and then I shared our story with her. I told very few people over the years, but in August 2002 my experience appeared in *Moments of Grace*, a quarterly spiritual magazine from author Neale Donald Walsch, who created the Conversations with God Foundation.

In 2008, during a visit from Joel, I mentioned that our story was in a magazine and showed him a copy. He then confessed what happened to him after we crashed into the wall and fell backwards into the water. Joel said that he went into the hole with me and soon found himself traveling up into a brilliant white light. He was met by a woman who told him that it was not his time yet and that he would have to return to Earth. He immediately left the light and found himself in the water, but not in the hole. In fact, he searched and couldn't find the hole. It would have been difficult to see because you had to look down at a dark riverbed through eighteen inches of moving water.

Eighteen years after our accident, Joel confessed that he had a near-death experience at the age of nine and was sent back by a Spirit to live out his life.

Two years later, in March 2010, Joel and I went to Portland, Oregon, to visit Chris for a weekend. We sat at the bar in a restaurant where Chris had worked for years and had a beer. Joel left us to use the restroom, and as he turned the corner, Chris lowered his head and sobbed uncontrollably. I was confused and worried, and I asked what was wrong.

"I found the hole," he said, looking into my eyes. "I found the edge of the hole, and I looked down and saw you, but I couldn't force myself to jump in and save you. I'm sorry." I calmed Chris and told him that it was OK. He wouldn't have been able to pull me out at the age of ten. He had carried this burden, his guilt, around for twenty years, and now it all came rushing out of him.

That's how traumatic this event, this miracle, was to our family. Terry and I didn't mention it for eleven years, Joel for eighteen, and Chris for twenty. We had a family near-death experience, and my life was saved by a miracle when, with my last conscious thought, I asked God, "Is that all You wanted from me?"

It has to be a miracle by every definition of the word. I traveled out of a hole in the river, upstream through rapids, and appeared, kneeling and choking, in front of two terrified witnesses. Terry, Chris, and Joel never saw me leave the hole. I didn't swim upstream through the small rapids and then crawl out onto the tip of the island in time to frighten two kayakers. I materialized from out of the blackness and onto the island.

At the moment of my death, I talked to God and got His answer. His Miracle saved my life. Of this, I have no doubt.

six
The Visit

⌒

My two visions of the brown car and the miracle in the river still were not enough to get me to take action and begin to look for answers. This time Spirit enlisted my mother's help to provide another experience and new information in order to get my attention.

Less than six months after my life was saved by God's miracle, my mother was dying of multiple myeloma cancer. When she was pronounced "day-to-day," I went to visit her in the hospital in Buffalo, New York. Mom was on a morphine drip to manage her pain and curled up in a fetal position on her bed. Most of my time with her, she was in a near-coma state. She could barely manage to say "yes" or "no," but she had a burst of energy when she saw recent photos of her grandsons. I stayed alone with her until late on my last night since I had an early flight back to Denver the next morning. Mom sat up, leaned against her pillows, and spoke clearly and excitedly about a visit from my dad who had died twenty-two years earlier. He was joined, in Spirit, by two of his brothers and a brother-in-law. She was thrilled to see them and to learn that she would be soon be joining them in Heaven. She told me that she saw Jesus at the foot of her bed and He spoke to her. She was amazed that anything like this was possible. I don't remember her exact words, and I must have been very surprised. I had never heard of anything like this.

A visit from deceased people whom you can see and hear and converse with? That's impossible, isn't it?

Yet here she was, far removed from her near-coma state. Mom said that she wasn't afraid to die any longer, and she even seemed to welcome it. After all of her pain and suffering, she was at peace with it. We had a good talk, and I left wondering if any of this could be true. I later shared Mom's words with her husband, Andy, at their home. I stood in the doorway of the guest room and said aloud, "Dad, if you're really here, give me a sign." In an instant, my suitcase, which had sat for days on a wooden chair, flipped up and over, then crashed to the floor. Very frightened, I ran from the room.

The next morning I returned to the hospital and knew this would be the last time I ever saw my mother alive. As I walked down the corridor, I overheard two nurses.

"Oh, my God! Have you seen Emily? Go take a look."

Farther on, I heard two doctors say those same words, and I hurried to her room. When I entered, I couldn't believe my eyes. Mom sat in a chair below the window. She wore a robe, her hair was combed, and she wore full makeup. Amazingly, she was her usual, feisty self, and not the cancer victim wasting away I had seen the past three days.

It was a wonderful, final visit. Looking back, I realize that it was a gift from God. I was allowed to see Mom for the final time as she always had been, and not in her current state. I wasn't dealing with her illness and imminent death very well. She retired from the U.S. Post Office in March and soon discovered she was very ill. Here, in the first week of December, she was pronounced day-to-day.

The last time I saw my Mom alive, she was her old self, and I treasure that. It had to be a gift, and brings tears to my eyes whenever I recall it. I realize how fortunate I am, compared to those who never had a chance to say good-bye or last saw their loved ones in an incapacitated state.

I left and called my sister at work. I told her what I'd seen and suggested that she hurry over. She couldn't leave her office until the end of the day, and when she arrived, Mom was back in bed in a fetal position and on the morphine drip again.

She went home under hospice care and passed away less than three weeks later. In the days before her passing, she saw Spirits in her room, waiting to guide her Home, and warned visitors to be careful not to walk into them or to bump the little girl who sat on the end of her bed.

The day Mom died, I said good-bye once more over the phone. I told her that I loved her, and that it was OK for her to let go. It was time to go to Heaven. Knowing that she was in touch with my Dad and others prior to her passing was a great relief to me. Her passing was instrumental in the start of my personal spiritual journey. Perhaps she experienced this pain and suffering to act as a catalyst for my spiritual education.

Mom has come through over two hundred times during my meditations over twenty-two years, and she has stopped by during phone sessions with psychic mediums. Mom stepped out of a group of Spirits, identified herself as Emily, pointed to her chest, and told the medium, "I'm number one," and "Everything is copacetic," as she always did when she joked around. I never told the medium my mother had passed. Mom came through with a warning about a bloody polyp in my colon that wouldn't be a problem, and she was absolutely right. Thanks, Mom.

In a span of thirteen months three life-altering events occurred that propelled me onto my spiritual journey. First came the two visions of the brown car that led to the rescue of a family of six. The second was the miracle that saved my life in the river, and the third was my Mom's excitement over seeing my father, family members, and Jesus, in Spirit, and her "mini-recovery" to ease my pain.

Something strange, yet fantastic, was happening in my life. I didn't know what it was, but I was determined to find some answers. The remaining chapters in Part One explain the steps I took along my path, not necessarily in chronological order. I often compare my journey to climbing the rungs of a ladder. With each successful step I yearned for more. I went from reading books to meditating, seeking help from a hypnotherapist, and eventually making contact with my Guardian Angels and Spirit Guides. After that, I attended conferences and workshops, and continued to have even more wonderful contact and amazing experiences with the Other Side. As you continue reading about the steps I have taken, I hope you realize that they weren't especially difficult or frightening. Spirit contact is filled with feelings and messages of love, and—in my history—much humor.

I'd like you to say to yourself, *"I can do this. All I have to do is try."* That's all I did, and I have more than two decades of wonderful experiences as a result.

As Terry often tells me, have a mind that is open to everything and attached to nothing. Spirit proffers this:

> *"Don't try to control every issue. Offer your*
> *insight and release it to God. Have faith."*

seven

Meditations, Travel In Heaven, and Automatic Writing

⌒

*"Have faith in your Angels.
Meditate more, worry less."*

Soon after my mother's passing, I read numerous books about death and spirituality, and I discovered meditation tapes. This chapter shares my earlier experiences, and I'd like you to notice how easy the steps are for you to follow.

Meditation

For years whenever I meditated using guided imagery tapes, I would lie on the bed and be perfectly still. As my mind and body relaxed, I became aware of tingling sensations in my fingertips that spread through my fingers. They would slowly spread apart and finally begin to lift. My hands and arms rose from my sides, going up and up, higher and higher, until I would sneak a groggy and squinty peek and see that both arms were fully extended and pointed towards the ceiling.

It seemed so weird. I had no control of my hands and arms—as if some spiritual energy source made them float up and away from my body. I meditated like that for at least five years, and often I would hold my arms straight up that way for twenty minutes of the twenty-five minute tape. As I progressed in my ability to get deeper more quickly—a fact that a few psychic mediums have been told by my Angels and Guides—the energy surrounding me seemed to grow stronger. For a few months my legs rose up along with my arms, and I'd lie in bed in a meditative state with a strong feeling that my four appendages reached for Heaven. I looked like a hospital patient in traction.

My eyes were always closed, and I would think, "Oh, this can't be good." I'd sneak a peek to confirm it, and I'd be right.

What the heck was going on? How can I possibly be doing this? And for twenty minutes at a time? Really? When the meditations ended, I'd have to wait a few minutes since my arms and legs were too numb to move.

What's next? Do I levitate off the bed? Do I float up to the ceiling like a helium-filled balloon and hope that a blade from the ceiling fan doesn't strike me?

I decided to stop meditating in bed. Instead, I would sit up straight in a chair and be grounded, and I could use a notebook and pen to write down what I saw and heard via automatic writing.

And that is exactly what I did. I no longer feared losing control of my limbs and lifting off the bed. Now I feared not being able to decipher the chicken-scratch notes I scribbled uncontrollably. I still do, but now I use a magnifying glass when needed. I wonder if anyone else has this same "uplifting experience." I don't recall ever reading or hearing about it.

Travel in Heaven

I prefer to use guided meditation tapes to help me relax and follow the step-by-step direction. Plus, there is an ending that snaps me back to reality in case I don't make contact and "crash" into an unplanned nap of thirty to sixty minutes.

As I "count down" into my relaxation, I imagine myself falling into a deep, dark tunnel. I zoom down in a free fall past the numbers being spoken on the tape and see myself in whatever clothes I have on at the time. Once I am sufficiently relaxed—if not I'll re-start the tape—the next section carries me upward as I zip through white clouds and perfectly clear, blue skies. When I "arrive," I burst through a bright, white light and discover where I am and who is waiting for me.

I have no control over this. I don't direct my mind to ensure a specific location to make sure I'm not imagining this. I just go with the flow.

Ever since I first met my Guardian Angels, David and Arianna, and my Spirit Guide, Dan, back in 1991, they have greeted me together. At first we met in beautiful meadows full of yellow flowers that swayed in a gentle breeze, or snowy, rocky mountaintops, which I didn't care for at all since I'm afraid of heights. Even though I'm on the Other Side, I still hold on to my fear of heights, because I'M JUST VISITING! I truly believe that the fact that I am not in a coma or clinically dead influences my more pedestrian perceptions of color, sights, and sounds. I am always escorted whenever multiple locations are involved and whisked away by the Speed of Thought—theirs, not mine. Make no mistake; I am always along for the ride. I'm a visitor at all times, and I never go anywhere alone.

Other locations I've visited and remember include:

An enormous Boulevard of gigantic white squares, depressed a bit in elevation in the center of a group of unbelievably beautiful buildings hundreds of feet away. I visit with my Angels and Guides.

My "School," a huge, old cathedral-like building with extremely high ceilings. It's empty except for small groups of Spirit Guides meeting with "visitors" like me.

Various Halls and Temples where I meet with teams of other Spirit Guides around long tables in simple "conference rooms," or with Dan, David, and Arianna in an open pod-like office that has a small, round table, even though we all stand. I can see innumerable other pods with seemingly infinite levels that look down upon an enormous "lobby." My friends stand with their backs to the half-wall that overlooks the "lobby," and I always stand with my back to the far wall for safety reasons—as if I could fall to my death while visiting Heaven.

The Hall of Records where I beg for a peek at the Akashic Records to try to cheat and find out what this life has in store for me. This is another "room" that seems to extend forever with levels that go on farther than I can see. I stand on a metallic walkway with lattice openings, and I can see hundreds of feet below—which does my heart absolutely no good.

A Healing Temple where I'm sent occasionally at the end of my sessions. I lie on a table, and Angels pass long, green rods over my body to help with various health issues. During my annual visit to my cardiologist a few years ago, all of my "numbers" were terrific. He said that he didn't know what I was doing, but I should keep doing it. I laughed because I knew that the only thing I was doing was asking for Healing Angels to visit me while I slept, and I was taken to the Healing Temple occasionally when I meditated. Otherwise, I just walked to the mailbox, and this wouldn't equate to terrific numbers.

Less than half of the time, family and friends pop in to say hello, if they are allowed. They appear off in the background or "step into frame" and request permission from my Angels to speak with me, usually near the end of a session. It's important to understand that I do not go into the meditation with a plan to spend time with specific Departed Loved Ones. It has never happened that way. I meditate to make contact with my Angels and Guides for guidance and information. Seeing DLOs is always a bonus.

There have been times when I've asked to see certain individuals, and my Angels will turn and look away, as if "sensing" what these individuals might be doing. I usually get a simple *"They're busy,"* and the discussion ends. Actually, there is no discussion. I ask questions and listen to whatever my Angels and Guides have to offer.

There have been a very few occasions when I have been in a large conference room with a distinguished Council, and I stand inside a U-shaped table while my Angels and Spirit Guide speak on my behalf in my plea to change my Sacred Contract or Chart and alter the goals I have chosen for this life. I am not allowed to hear any of their conversations, and the solemnness and importance of these meetings are overwhelming. I won't say I'm scared, but I am certainly intimidated.

Automatic Writing

Automatic writing occurs when you write down detailed messages received from the Other Side. In my case, when I meditate, I sit upright with a notebook on my lap or on the arm of my easy chair. I close my eyes, listen to a meditation tape, and loosely hold a pen. Then, when I make contact with my Angels and Guides, the words begin to flow, and my scribbling, or automatic writing, begins. My hand moves quickly and haphazardly across the pages, and I am able to turn to a new page when I need to. I believe my personal record length is six pages of notes. I rely on these written notes since I remember only about half of what I hear during these sessions.

However, after all these years, I can never easily read my notes. I write in longhand, and then I review and print the messages above or next to the words. I usually need a magnifying glass to decipher my chicken scratches. At times days have gone by as I stare at jumbled messes of words in overlapping sentences before I am able to decipher their meaning. I ask myself, "What the heck could that possibly be?" Then words pop into my head. Sometimes. If I'm really stuck, I draw a line or a space where the "lost" words belong and come back to it days later. A fresh set of eyes usually does the trick, and I soon know what's missing. Other times I flat out beg for help.

The manner of speech in these messages is quite formal and concise, very different from the way I speak or write, and they often refer to me as "Dear Paul" when they want to accentuate a specific point. I have never referred to myself as "Dear Paul" and would never have considered it, as has everyone I've ever known.

The messages I receive are very personal, and I'll attempt to share some whenever possible. I've discovered that when I check them months—or even years—later, the information is very accurate. For example, during a meditation I asked if our "eight-hundred-pound-gorilla" agent in Hollywood was going to sell my latest screenplay that he was very excited about. He had phoned me with his plans when he read the last page. Well, it was sent out for a "weekend read" but didn't sell on Monday. In my meditation I heard "he's going to dump it for you," meaning a quick sale for less-than-hoped-for money. It's an option we decided against on another project years before that was a big mistake. Either I heard it wrong or translated my scribbled notes incorrectly because after an unpleasant meeting with my then-writing partner, he didn't dump the script, he dumped us! At least I got the "dump" part right.

I read somewhere that doodling circles is the Spirit's way of greeting you. My school notebooks throughout my life are filled with Slinky-esque doodles, as are my personal journals and screenplay notes.

I first wrote this section in a notebook while I was sitting at one end of our dining room table, and I had asked my Angels and Guides to help me remember my experiences. I finished and looked around the house, and two feet to my right a small white orb, the size of a tennis ball, slowly rose from the floor about three feet up, glided away from me, and then disappeared behind a chair, tucked in at the center of the table.

"Did I just see an orb?" I said aloud. Instantly, the orb returned. It slowly floated from behind the chair and towards me before it dropped and vanished back into the carpet. I took it as a confirmation that my automatic writing is indeed influenced by the Other Side.

Now did any of that seem too difficult for you? You simply relax, clear your mind, and meditate, with or without a tape. Before I make any attempt at contact, I ask God for His help and protection. At times absolutely nothing happens, and I accept that since I believe the failure to make a connection is my fault. I view any information, guidance, and visits as gifts, and I humbly accept them as such.

Be open to receiving Spirit, and when you're comfortable with it, begin taking notes. Trust that the Spirit's guidance will come, and be prepared to practice for weeks, months, and even years. It's worth it. Remember that your Angels, Guides, and DLOs have waited patiently for your attempt to welcome them into your life. Are you ready to try? Not yet?

Then continue reading, and see what other types of communication that you may be missing but that I'm not.

eight
Spirit Guides

I describe a Spirit Guide as a best friend on the Other Side who chooses to remain in Heaven while we experience our latest incarnation. They are constantly with us to keep us on track with the chart we've written and the goals we hope to achieve in this lifetime. Think of your best friend here on Earth—someone who knows you best—your hopes, fears, dreams, issues, likes and dislikes, your secrets, talents, skills, etc. Let's pretend it's fifty years in the future, and the two of you have reconnected in Heaven. You decide to reincarnate to take another shot at the life you always dreamt of living, only now you've evolved spiritually and choose an even more difficult series of lessons. You want your best friend to reincarnate with you to support you on this wonderful, new journey, but your friend says, "No, thanks. I'm good here in Heaven."

"But you're my best friend; you have to come with me. It'll be fun. I'm going to be born into a dysfunctional family with all kinds of abuse and health issues, have three horrible relationships, and then move to an impoverished nation and work in health care until I join the rebels and fight for freedom. I may or may not be executed by a firing squad. We'll work that out later. Are you in?"

Then your best friend stares at you with more sympathy than understanding because you appear to have lost your mind, learned absolutely nothing, and he/she really enjoys being in Heaven. Another go-around on our planet isn't in the stars. Your friend has signed up for painting lessons with Da Vinci and Rembrandt, lectures from Confucius, Socrates, and Benjamin Franklin, and has tickets for the dueling pianos concert of Beethoven/Mozart versus Liberace/Ray Charles. Even better, your friend says he/she will stay and train to become a Spirit Guide—perhaps even your Spirit Guide. He/she will assist you with your new chart and be with you every step of the way on your latest physical journey. You can still be best friends, only you won't remember any of it—unless you choose to develop your spirituality and eventually become aware of his/her presence.

Your best friend will be with you every step of the way to offer love, support, and guidance. It's just that they'll be commuting between Heaven and Earth, and you will be here wondering why your life is so gosh darn hard.

Spirit Guides communicate with us by putting information directly into our minds. We can call it instinct, but I believe Guides are whispering in our ears, and if we're in danger, they shout clear warnings. They may come and go, working with us on various phases of our lives, or on specific projects and experiences, or lessons we need to learn. Spirits are people who have lived on Earth, and they become Guides if they choose to train—and then help—those of us presently experiencing incarnations in order to advance the development of their own souls.

In the spring of 1991, I purchased meditation tapes and within a few weeks I fortunately had success in connecting with Spirits on the Other Side and recalling memories from past lives.

The first time I made contact, I lay in bed as I listened to the guided meditation. When I "arrived," I found myself in a wooded area on a beautiful sunny day, but the sky seemed to be a creamy color instead of blue. I stood near a shallow stream, and across the water an attractive young woman reclined on a long rock maybe forty feet away. She wore a flowery, summer dress with a matching floppy hat. She was barefoot and said her name was Florence. In an instant a map of Kentucky flashed before me with the city of the same name highlighted. That was odd, I thought.

Florence assured me that this was real, and I had made contact with the Other Side, or Heaven. Florence stayed on the rock and spoke softly so I wouldn't be frightened. She was very nice and friendly, and she answered my questions as I stood on my side of the stream and looked around in amazement. I was stunned but not frightened. I knew I was safe in my bed, but I was also "there" with Florence. There was a disconnect between my body and soul, and I realized this during my very first contact.

My body lay motionless on my bed at home, but my unconscious—or Spirit or soul—was definitely far away in a wonderfully peaceful place. I remember this vividly but cannot recall the details of our conversation, except that it felt as real as it could possibly be. When the meditation tape ended, I slept for hours, and that would be the norm for the first six months of using the tapes. I felt physically and mentally exhausted for two or three days afterwards. Whatever was happening, I had accessed a part of my mind that I hadn't before, and my body was having a physical reaction to it.

I don't recall ever speaking with Florence again. Perhaps this was her only assignment—to welcome me and make me feel comfortable on my very first spiritual journey Home.

My personal Spirit Guide is a really funny and playful character named Dan. Actually, when we first met, he said, "My name's Sennodan, but you can call me Dan."

He first appeared to me in a meditation as a morbidly obese Middle Eastern man sitting cross-legged on the floor in a white robe. He laughed loudly, obviously amused with my discomfort.

I told him that his appearance didn't work for me, and he immediately changed it, revealing himself as the actor John Goodman, who played "Dan" Conner in the television series *Roseanne*. For the next ten years that's how Dan appeared to me, then he began representing himself as a classier, handsome, very tall figure with long golden hair and wearing a white robe.

Dan is quite the jokester. In the 1990s I'd see a psychic once a year for entertainment purposes, of course, and seven different psychics in a row started the session by saying, "There's a man standing behind your right shoulder, and he says his name is Dan." A couple of the psychic mediums I've talked with multiple times really enjoy Dan and his energy, humor, and roguish spirit. Pun intended.

When I meditate, he's always there with my two Guardian Angels to give me guidance and answer my questions. He has introduced me to various Spirit Guides who have worked with me over the years. He is truly a best friend, and I always beg him to reveal himself to me in physical form.

I came close once. I sat at the desk in our home office reading my Tarot cards. I heard a voice say, *"Look at the television,"* so I turned to look over my left shoulder. As I did, the broadcast shut off, and the screen went black, and I saw instead the reflection of a man standing behind my right shoulder. I immediately swung back around to look, but there was no one behind me, just the bookcase to my right.

Then I swung back around in my chair, gazed at the television once again, and there he was—standing behind my right shoulder. His reflection cut the bookcase in half. I spun once again with the same result, and yet again, until I finally realized that this was Dan's idea of fun. So I quit.

Over the past twenty-two years Dan has undoubtedly been the cause of what I term little "hellos" from my Angels and Guides—all the missing items, moving objects, electrical issues, etc. As I type, I'm reminded that when I used to watch Colorado Rockies' games on television from my easy chair—barefoot and in shorts with one ankle crossed over the knee of the other leg—"someone" would grab my big toe, pull hard, and straighten my leg until I slid out of the chair onto the floor.

Yeah, Dan's a fun guy. My Spirit Guide is the best invisible friend and caretaker I could ever hope for. As I typed that last sentence, I could hear his voice in my head dictating it to me. I kid you not.

For years and years in the 1990s, I was going to "School" while I meditated. I met with a group of thirteen Spirit Guides who stood around me in a semicircle while I sat on a low, curved wooden chair. We were in a large, cathedral-like building with many groups like mine, and other visiting individuals like me, sitting on these same chairs. The Spirit Guides communicated telepathically, infusing me with some knowledge that I trust has been—and will be—important to my spiritual advancement.

Over the years I've met many Guides. I once drove down a road and saw a sign for a Psychic Fair, and I stopped in. I sat down for a reading from a man who had an "Angel Readings" sign on his table. He lowered his head and closed his eyes as he "prepared" himself. When he was ready, he looked up and beyond me, and his eyes suddenly grew wide with fear.

"You've got nineteen Angels behind you."

"Yeah, want to know their names?"

He was unnerved, to say the least.

Over the years I've met even more Spirit Guides, led by David F. With his round glasses and mop-top yellow hair, he resembles singer John Denver, and he helps me with my writing projects. Whenever we meet during a meditation, I am whisked to a simple conference room with a large table surrounded by chairs. Usually ten or more Guides are present, and they bombard me with scene ideas and dialogue changes. I scribble their "notes" as fast as I can, using my Automatic Writing "skills." It's either that or "work visits" at three a.m.

In attendance at these meetings is King Vidor, who is mentioned elsewhere as the *"distinguished"* film director. As I typed that sentence, a Spirit behind me instructed me to add, "distinguished." My son, Joel, pointed out that King Vidor has a star on the Hollywood Walk of Fame, and he took a photo of it for me. So "distinguished" it is.

I was at a "Celebrate Your Life" conference in Scottsdale, Arizona, in November 2011 with my wife, Terry. Since 2000, we've attended these wonderful conferences, put on by Mischka Productions, to see our favorite authors and speakers give workshops on spiritual topics.

During a guided meditation session with English psychic medium Lisa Williams, Dan came through and said it's finally time for me to see my Akashic Record. In an instant, I was there and thrilled that after twenty years of trying, this was the moment I'd been waiting for—the answer to what's in store for me in this life. I reached for the book and removed it from the shelf. It's large and awkward, and I eagerly opened it, only to see BLANK PAGES! Page after page of absolutely nothing. Dan laughed hysterically. I turned to him, grimaced, and was whisked back to my chair in the large ballroom. He really got me good. Dan, the Jokester from Heaven.

An amazing thing happened during this workshop with Lisa Williams. She asked the crowd if we wanted to see her Spirit Guides, and we all eagerly said yes. Who wouldn't? She climbed atop a large folding table on the left end of the stage. Behind her was a giant screen used to show the keynote speakers in the evenings. The screen was a royal blue. Lisa stood on the table and opened her arms wide, expanding her aura. She asked her Guides to show themselves, and they did.

It didn't take long before three Spirit Guides arrived onscreen behind her. A large, whitish man-shaped figure appeared behind her left shoulder as some in the audience gasped and yelled out what they saw. Some people saw the Spirits, and some didn't. This Spirit "jumped" from side-to-side behind Lisa as she spoke, as if saying, *"Here I am. Can you see me? Now I'm over here."* He did it repeatedly. Then, up in the left corner, two more Spirits appeared, standing very close together. These two appeared to be feminine shapes, and they didn't move at all. They just stood and watched. There were no visible features, just heads, shoulders, and torsos of white energy.

For those audience members who could see them, it was amazing, and for those who couldn't, very disappointing.

I suffered a serious heart attack in August 2000. As the doctors encouraged me to stay conscious, I decided that I was going to escape the pain by beginning my meditation process. I recited the calming words, repeating them over and over— *"twenty, twenty, twenty... down, down, down..."* and in moments I could "see" my Spirit Guides and Angels encircling the operating theater. Some smiled and nodded while others gave me a "thumbs up," and I knew I would survive.

I recently had a phone conversation with my son, Chris, and he was going through a low period. I offered to ask my Angels, Guides, and parents in Spirit to help and give him an unmistakable sign. We said goodbye, and in a few minutes he felt overwhelmed, laughing and crying uncontrollably, and then he passed out on his bed. Spirit Guides really made their presence known to him.

Are you curious about who your Spirit Guides are—your Heavenly best friends? Are you ready to meditate, ask their names, and discover what areas of your life they help you with? Or are you feeling safe and comfortable on this rung of your ladder?

Maybe later? Fine, let's continue then. I've also had experiences with Spirits visiting our house. Not the Spirit Guides who work with me and have a hand in my contract and spiritual growth, but visiting Spirits that I call "Looky-Loos."

nine

Looky-Loos

"It was a Spirit Guide posing as Terry, not to play a trick on you. It was a little hello from your team, to let you know that we are with you."

A psychic healer told me a few years ago that because of my spirituality, I emit a light that those on the Other Side can see, and some come to investigate. I believe that they arrive, see that it's just me, and leave, disappointed. I find their visits frightening and frustrating. I asked my Angels and Spirit Guide to stop them from coming unless they are going to interact with me. I want guidance, not voyeurs.

I was watching television on the living room sofa and looked over at the front door where a young man was standing and looking at a clipboard he held. He had a nearly-shaved head and a very short beard, and he wore a patchwork robe of red and green. He turned his head a little to the right and jotted something on his clipboard. He was as solid as any human, but suddenly he broke apart into thousands of tiny balls of golden light and disappeared. I shivered, closed my eyes, and turned away for a few seconds. *Did I just see that?* When I looked back at the television, one of my favorite episodes of *Frasier* had just started, and I immediately calmed down.

On another evening while watching television from the sofa, I turned as I tried to get comfortable and spotted a young man with red hair and a goatee as he sat on the floor and smiled at me. He was on the other side of my ottoman, in front of the television. I screamed—hey, it happens sometimes—and he scooted on his butt across the floor until he disappeared behind an arm of our L-shaped sofa. I got up and searched, but of course, there was no one there. Years later during a meditation, I learned that it was Terry's brother, Brian, who had passed over fifteen years earlier and whom I had met only once for a few hours. His story appears elsewhere.

One night I came to bed late, and Terry was already asleep. I slept on the side by the window, and she slept on the side near the door and master bath. After thirty seconds of facing the window, I decided to shift my position and turned to lie on my back.

As I did, I noticed Terry walking out of the bathroom towards the bed. I didn't say anything, since we both have trouble getting back to sleep once we are awake, and closed my eyes. In a second I heard snoring from the pillow next to me, flipped my hand over, and accidently smacked Terry in the face. What? How could Terry be snoring in bed next to me when she was walking from the bathroom to the bed?

My eyes sprung open, and I sat up halfway and turned towards her. To my utter shock, I saw, standing next to the bed, a blonde woman in a dark blue robe. She leaned over and stared at Terry, fast asleep. This woman had weird L-shaped hair that appeared to be as stiff as wood. It was parted at the back of her head, and half of it went down her neck, and the other half came forward to her brow. I didn't scream, but I covered my eyes and let out a quiet "Whoa." She was only a few feet away. I took a peek five seconds later, and she was gone.

But it wasn't for long.

The next week I once again came to bed late, and Terry was already asleep. Within thirty seconds I shifted and turned towards the center of the bed. Standing near the doorway, next to our big-screen television, was the Blonde Spirit. This time she brought a friend—a tall, attractive Brunette Spirit, who was wearing a dark red robe. They both stared at Terry from across the room and exchanged whispers. I sat upright in bed and stared in silence. The two Spirits noticed me and seemed surprised. The Blonde turned left and headed towards the bathroom. The Brunette turned right, passed the television, and headed towards the dresser.

After three steps both broke apart into tiny balls of golden light that quickly extinguished. I collapsed back onto the bed and pulled a pillow over my head. But I didn't scream. I'm getting better. I told these stories to a psychic, and she laughed and said that it was Terry's husband and a friend from one of her past lives. They had stopped by to check on her. I was not happy and insisted, demanded, begged, and pleaded with my Angels and Guides to please keep these Looky-Loos away.

Unfortunately, it was not to be. I was cooking at the stove one day, and suddenly my head swiveled to the right as a black Shadow Person crossed the dining room and the living room, before disappearing into the home office with our two cats, Mabel and Millie, in hot pursuit.

The Shadow Person looked like wispy, black smoke—maybe five-and-a-half-feet tall. I didn't see a face, and it moved away quickly.

I hurried out of the kitchen and avoided Mabel when she hit the brakes and refused to go any further. The Shadow Person turned the corner and disappeared into the office with Millie just a few feet behind. I reached the doorway seconds later and looked inside. The room was empty except for a very confused Millie, who turned in circles as she looked for her prey.

Our son, Joel, was visiting a few years ago and was eating breakfast at the counter. Suddenly he yelled, "Did you just see that? A black shadow just walked past the doorway of your bedroom." I ran in to take a look, but there was nothing there. I'm sure Joel saw a black, wispy, smoky Shadow Person, just as I had.

About five years ago on a beautiful Saturday morning I was in our master bathroom and looked through the bedroom and out an open window at our yard, the field and farm beyond, and the distant treetops and canyon wall. The nice view was interrupted as someone in a long, white robe—like the ancient Romans and Greeks wore—dashed past the doorway. About Terry's size and with the same short, brown hair, he was gone in an instant. I remember that I didn't see any feet, and at that speed there was no way he wouldn't have crashed into the desk in the corner of the bedroom. So what's going on here?

I raced into the bedroom, and there was no one there. I hurried into the living room and found Terry sleeping on the sofa and wearing a mint-green lounging outfit, so it couldn't have been her.

It was another Spirit sighting with no interaction, and while they really aren't scary as in horror films, they are annoying to me. If I'm able to see you in my home, could you at least say something? Is that too much to ask?

I've had two partial Spirit sightings in our new house. The first took place in the living room as I sat on the sofa and read the newspaper. On the ottoman before me, our cat, Mabel, reacted suddenly, swinging her head around to stare at the built-in shelves between the big screen TV and the fireplace. Her sudden movement and the way she crouched with her neck and head sticking out and her ears raised told me she had seen something. It was how all four cats we've adopted since 1987 react when they see something that only they can see.

A second later I saw it, too. Reflected in the glass cover of the gas fireplace, a pair of legs wearing pants walked past us. I saw their reflection clearly, but there was no man to be seen walking through the living room. Mabel followed the sight with her gaze and then ran and hid under a bed. I sat there, upset by another Looky-Loo encounter.

Another partial sighting happened in August 2011. I was asleep in our bed in the middle of the night when the reading lamp on the desk next to me began to turn on and off. Its flexible neck was turned so that the halogen bulb pointed directly at my face. I awoke, confused, and saw the ugliest pair of red plaid pants ever. They looked like red golf pants with black-and-white squares. All I saw were the legs of whoever was standing there playing with the light. In a few seconds I realized what was happening, so I jerked back with a little "whoa" and covered my head with a pillow. The light stopped going on and off, and after a minute or an hour of pure fear, I saw that the Spirit was gone. Thanks for waking me up to show me your hideous pants, pal.

When Terry and I had a small group session in Denver with psychic medium Rebecca Rosen, Bob, Terry's dad, came through and told Rebecca he's laying down his golf clubs and said he's not into golf. Months later, during a meditation, Bob came through and told me that he had been the one playing with the lights in the bedroom. The first thing I thought was that if he's not into golf, why is he wearing the ugliest golf pants in Heaven and Earth? And why not present himself so I can see and communicate with him? Maybe these little "hellos" are all Looky-Loos can do, but after many years of this, it does get frustrating.

There have been many other sightings over the years, but mostly when I turn and catch a quick glimpse of someone, I wonder if I saw anything at all.

In June 2012, after I broke my leg and ankle and tore ligaments and tendons, I had surgery and spent two months on my back with my left foot and leg propped up on pillows. I took pain pills to combat the pain, and, combined with ice packs and elevation, I managed the pain quite well.

During the period I was taking pain pills, I did have a few sightings that I want to share with you, with my complete understanding that the strength and numbers of my medication may have had something to do with seeing them. But in my heart, and after reading my journal, I truly believe these were not drug-induced hallucinations but visits from Spirit.

Post-surgery, I saw myself in an all-white room with three huge test-tube holding pans on an oval track. In the holes were clear test tubes, either a squiggly T-shape or ones shaped like a hockey stick with the blade at the top. I can see two-dimensional men and women trapped inside these tubes. In the background, voices yelled out surnames while other voices shouted replies:

"Take him back. He's not ready. He can go. He's staying. He's going back into battle."

Battle? That one caught my attention, and my eyes sprung open. I was awake and in the hospital's recovery room with other patients. Nurses called out surnames just as I had heard before.

The response, *"He's going back into battle,"* made me wonder if I had been in a waiting room for souls, and we had been taken there for safety reasons or something else.

Three weeks later while meditating, I jotted down this explanation from my Angels:

"Yes, the waiting room was real. Souls can escape the trauma of the body and reenergize here with us in Heaven. The souls going back into battle were returning to a firefight in Afghanistan."

In the first two weeks after surgery, I would be awakened during the night by what appeared to be new Spirit Guides by my bed—two at the foot of the bed by the corners and two along the sides. They were young men in their early twenties, and they talked nervously about caring for me, asking questions like what they should do when my leg and foot shifted off my pillows or a bag of ice slipped off my ankle.

I remember groggily telling them, "Shut up; I'm trying to sleep." That surprised the heck out of them. *"He knows we're here!"* I had subsequent conversations with two of them while the other two remained silent.

During this period I woke up at six a.m. one day and noticed a golden object hovering in the corner of the bedroom. It had two sections and looked like an upside-down Stanley Cup for you hockey fans. Once I sat up in bed and took a good, hard look at it, it vanished.

I spent most of every day that first two weeks on the living room sofa so I could read, watch TV, and nap. Plus, the kitchen and bathroom were nearby, and I had my friend's life-saving scooter to use. I fell twice on my crutches in the first half hour, and I swore I wouldn't use them again.

One afternoon I awoke from a nap and saw a man walk across the living room and into the dining room before he vanished.

On another afternoon I dozed on the sofa and was awakened by the sounds of people talking. With my eyes half open, I lifted my head and saw eight men and women as they spoke and laughed in the dining room and kitchen. I heard the crack of pool balls coming from the kitchen—a strange sound because we don't have a pool table in our kitchen—but when I peeked, I saw a man with a pool stick lean over to line up his shot. The pool table was blocked by our breakfast bar, and I remember the other players laughed at his shot.

Later I had the sense that someone was very close to me, and then a woman started speaking to me. I opened my eyes, and there she was—a short woman with brown hair and glasses. She was leaning over the back of the sofa about two feet from my face. That freaked me out. I shut my eyes and grabbed a pillow to hide behind. When I gathered the courage to look, everyone was gone.

I see in my journal that I wrote those notes on 6/27/2012, and when I meditated the next day, here's what my Angels said:

"Yes, you are beginning to see Spirit Guides more easily as part of your advancement. Do not doubt the experience. You can communicate with them as you sleep and remember some of what they say. Have no doubt; they are with you to guard you during this period in your life. Your healing is going well. There will not be any problems or follow-up surgery, so ease your mind."

I had no problems or follow-up surgery, just a very long recovery so far. I include these Spirit Guides in the Looky-Loos section to point out the difference. After surgery, Spirits were sent to look after me, while otherwise they pop-in just to gawk at me or Terry. If my pain medication caused these experiences, why wouldn't my Angels, after twenty-one years, have told me so? I'm just saying.

Recently, the sightings have changed. Since I repeatedly tell my Angels and Spirit Guide that I'm not interested in seeing Looky-Loos, they changed the game so they can apparently still say their little "hellos" and have some fun with me.

I walked out of our home office into the living room and paused at the sofa to pet our cat Millie as she sat and watched the birds feeding outside. Out of the corner of my eye I caught a glimpse of Terry, fresh from the shower and in her birthday suit, as she raced past the bedroom doorway towards the dresser.

Thinking that this would be a great time to say good morning, I rushed over, entered the bedroom, and turned to the right, expecting to see her at the dresser. Wrong. She wasn't there. No one was.

I turned to my left, and looked through our long master-bath and into the walk-in closet. I spotted Terry, at least twenty-five feet away - and she was dressed.

So who did I see dash past the bedroom door that looked exactly like my wife?

It happened again a few weeks later. Terry had gone to bed to read and I was in the living room watching television. During a commercial, I went into our long, galley kitchen and spotted Terry in her baby blue pajamas with little sheep as she walked quickly from the laundry room and down the short hall before she disappeared behind the wall.

I hurried around the breakfast bar to intercept her because she must be going to the guest bedroom or the bathroom. Both rooms were dark as I approached, and I wondered how she got past me without my noticing and why she didn't say anything. I searched both rooms, but there was no sign of Terry so I hustled over to the master bedroom, opened the door, and there she was— fast asleep in bed in her blue jammies. I was tricked again by Spirits disguised as my wife.

Come on, who wouldn't recognize their spouse in their own home from fifteen feet away? Twice! There you have it. I complain about Looky-Loos, and for my trouble I get to see perfect Wife-Clones instead. I just can't win.

From my meditation notes:

"Spirits who visit you have no place with your destiny. We will monitor their visits... we are keeping you safe from Looky Loos. Don't worry, you'll see us first."

So far I haven't seen any more Looky-Loos or Spirits pretending to be my wife, and I'm OK with that. However, I do have Spirits, most from my "Team," who check in on me, and others who are merely curious. I've learned that being able to see Spirits as easily as I see human beings is an integral part of my spiritual growth and destiny. While seeing these Looky-Loos are another rung on my personal ladder, I truly prefer formal introductions from my Angels and Guides.

ten

Regressions

At this point it would be fair to say that you probably have an understanding of past lives and reincarnation. From all of my readings and experiences, I believe that our soul is eternal, and we experience a number of lifetimes in various time periods, locations, family groups, etc., in order to learn and grow. All of these efforts are dedicated to God.

As I've read many times, we are spiritual beings having a physical experience. We pass from this life and return Home—to Heaven— where we are reunited with loved ones from this and other lives. We rest, rejuvenate, study, and prepare ourselves to help others as Guides or to return for another incarnation.

While you don't have to believe in Heaven, past lives, or reincarnation, once you begin experiencing them, you simply can't deny it. You just "know" it is real, and, while no proof is really necessary, it sure would be nice.

When I first began meditating, I purchased a regression tape and had success making contact almost immediately. I believe I fell into a deep slumber the first couple of times since I relaxed so deeply. Psychic mediums tell me that my Angels mention how I am able to go under deeply and quickly.

I would lie on my bed and listen to the tape, and the first time I was successful, I found myself back in Kentucky in what I believe was the 1840s. I say "back" because I lived there briefly in 1983–1984. In my mind's eye, I saw myself as an older man with white hair and a ruddy face. One of my three sons had just married, and I walked through the celebration, through two rooms of a home or tavern, and took it all in. Guests were dressed in their best clothes, and they sang, danced, laughed, and drank. Suddenly, one of my sons—a young man with a tankard in hand—turned and spoke directly to me. I was startled since up until then I had been an observer moving through the action. I snapped out of the meditation and jumped up, frightened.

Another regression meditation earlier in that lifetime in Kentucky showed me as a younger man, around twenty, riding a prancing white horse across a meadow on my way to court the pretty young woman who would become my wife.

This was the first experience I shared with Terry during one of our after-dinner walks. We later visited Louisville, Kentucky, and took tours of a plantation and historic home. I immediately felt that I had been to both places before since they seemed so familiar and comfortable.

After being frightened when my son addressed me in the meditation, I used the services of a hypnotherapist in Denver. During my initial visit I told her of my experiences with light bulbs exploding as I passed by, and radios turning on unexpectedly. As I mentioned the radios, one that sat at the end of her desk turned itself on, and music began to play. She laughed and said she believed me.

She later helped me regress, and I saw my life as a young woman in a town I knew was in South Dakota. I got the impression that the year was 1873. I was crossing the dirt street with my two young children, a boy and a girl. A commotion down the street caught my attention— a bank had just been robbed. Men on horseback were shooting guns and heading our way. I tried to protect my children as we ran from the scene, and I'm struck by a bullet and killed instantly. My widowed husband was left to raise the children alone. In this life I have a real sense of dread whenever I see armored trucks and an intense fear of being in the wrong place at the wrong time.

The following week I was called to my son's elementary school for a meeting with his teacher. She was very concerned about a paper Joel wrote for class. It told the story of a young boy growing up in the Old

West. His mother was killed, and he and his sister were raised by an abusive father. Joel was nine years old and had composed seven hand-written pages on both sides. The story seemed to flow out of him. I stood in the hallway outside the classroom with the teacher and read the paper. I quickly grew excited, and this confused her.

"This is the story I told the hypnotherapist last week. I want a copy to show my wife. This is amazing." It was not the reaction the teacher had expected, and she appeared shocked by my enthusiasm.

I had not shared the story with Joel, but perhaps the story was out in the Universe. He picked up on it, and his subconscious memories of this past life came forward simultaneously.

In that past life, I was the mother who was shot, and my ex-wife was the father in Joel's story. In this incarnation, I am the father, and she is the mother, and this is another attempt for me to raise my sons, and for her to be a better parent. We divorced in 1983, when the boys were almost two and three years old. I received sole custody, allowing me to be the parent I believe that I missed out on being a century earlier.

Later that year, Joel and a classmate were very excited when they came home. They had seen a filmstrip that day about the Old West, and it had shown a young couple who they insisted looked exactly like my ex-wife and me.

I visited Joel's class once and spoke about writing. The class had gone on a trip to Cripple Creek, an old mining town. I asked the students what old playground equipment they saw, but no one spoke up. I did a simple regression exercise then so the kids could clear their minds and revisit the playground, and the room was filled with excited kids, eyes closed, as they shouted out all they now saw in their minds' eyes. It was very successful, and I suggested the teacher try it herself to help the students focus, yet somehow I doubt the school district allowed hypnosis on children.

I am less interested in my past lives than I am with my future, so I always ask for a peek at my Sacred Contract or Chart and Akashic Records. I remember using the regression tape one day to see if I could discover why I have certain lifelong fears. These are the questions I asked:

"Why am I afraid of heights?"

I quickly saw myself as a fifteen-year-old Native American boy, looking out at a mountain vista in Arizona. I stepped onto a small rock ledge high above a canyon to watch a beautiful sunset. I've always loved sunsets, especially when the boys and I lived on the Gulf Coast in Florida, where we would go across the street to the beach to enjoy their beauty or sometimes I would watch them through a window while sitting on my bed.

As the Indian boy, I stood on the ledge and held my spear in my right hand. I looked down at my bare, dark feet and saw the thin ledge crack behind my heels, and then I felt the sudden sensation of falling. I was quickly pulled away from that memory to avoid seeing my death.

Now, waiting in a dark place and still in the meditation I asked myself, "Why am I afraid of water?"

Whisked away to a ship being tossed in a storm at night, I saw I was in the 1700s, and I was a blond-haired, ten-year-old cabin boy in the British Navy. It was my first voyage, and I excitedly ran up on deck to experience the storm. I didn't see any sailors on deck. I held onto anything I could to keep my balance and then look up to see a monstrous wave crash down on me before I'm swept overboard. I didn't have a drowning sensation when the cabin boy disappeared into the night, but I found myself back in the darkness. A quick side story - I took a cruise to the Bahamas in 1976 and ran up on deck during a severe storm when I was alone in the movie theater watching *The Way We Were* and found myself swaying in my seat. This time I remembered to hold onto anything I could before I realized how dangerous it was and I retreated to my cabin. Fool me once...

"Why am I afraid of being out in Nature?"

I've never been an outdoors type of guy. Our family didn't do that. I've been camping twice in my life. The first time I turned my ankle trying to help Terry set-up the tent, and couldn't sleep because I felt every stone and rock through the sleeping bag. The second time I tried to camp, we took a hike on an old loggers' trail and got caught in a thunder-and-lightning storm. We hurried back to our tent, deep in the woods, as sheets of lightning flashed on both sides of us. I repeatedly asked my Angels to get us out of there safely and fortunately we did, but it was a terrifying experience.

I next saw myself as a little boy of eight or nine, alone on a trail through heavy woods. It's a medieval period from my look and the feel. I think it's Germany. I stopped and looked up the trail when I heard something approach.

Soldiers on horseback rode past in armor and helmets without visors, and I'm thrilled to see them up close. They raced past in single file, and I backed off the trail just a bit. Some smiled at me, but as the last soldier got close, he grinned, lifted his large sword and swung it down towards my head as he rode past. Everything went black, and I was whisked away.

I asked my subconscious for answers to these fears and received information I never would have expected nor had any reason to. So where did it come from? It came from within me. I listened with my soul and an open heart. I was open to receive information and saw myself in past lives, and I believe that you can as well.

I've attended workshops with author Dr. Brian Weiss, known as America's leading authority on past-life regression therapy. Dr. Weiss says that two-thirds of attendees at his workshops remember experiences from previous lifetimes.

In my regressions with him, I seem to always die quickly and come out of the regression early on, and if it occurs during a workshop I always feel cheated because the other participants, always in the hundreds, are having fuller experiences. I'm left looking around the ballroom as I sit in silence and wait for the session to end.

Here's a sampling of my brief past-life regressions:

I saw myself as a Native American teenager in New Mexico, and feel that the period is the late 1600s. My village is under attack from another tribe trying to steal our food supply. About sixteen, I wear a loincloth and have long, black hair. I rise from behind a low wall and throw my spear at our attackers, but I'm immediately struck in the chest by an arrow and die. I felt the pain in my chest and regretted it all instantly.

In Peru, during the time of the Incas, I am a captain of the royal guards, killed by one of my men out of his jealousy of my position. He later kills my wife and two sons in our simple home to cover it up.

In a lifetime in what appears to be Atlantis, I saw myself drinking from a goblet of wine, in a hallway in a business environment. In seconds, I slump against a wall and die, poisoned by coworkers threatened by my abilities.

In Mexico, I see myself as a foreman during the construction of one of the pyramids, coordinating the transport of large blocks of stone. I live in a small hut with my wife and our baby son, and we are very happy together. In this regression I didn't see my death. Finally, a happy life!

As a fifteen-year-old boy in a small Massachusetts village, I carry buckets of water on a yoke across my shoulders from a stream. It is hot, tiresome work and I see a scene where I hate plucking feathers from dead chickens. It has to be the mid-1770s because I see myself with three British soldiers outside a barn. They laugh at me, and when I call them lobsterbacks, one runs me through with a bayonet and I die. They escape and go unpunished.

I had this regression with the Denver psychotherapist because I remember that later in this session with her, as this same boy, I walked into a tavern filled with boisterous men as they drank and laughed. I walked through the crowd and realized that no one could see or hear me, no matter what I did. My hypnotherapist told me that I was a ghost and didn't realize it. It was a very confusing time for this boy as he wandered around the village trying to get someone to notice him.

During my regressions with this hypnotherapist, while she spoke and led me on guided meditations, my subconscious was steps ahead of her, anticipating her directions. She'd ask why I was frowning and I'd tell her that she was too slow and that I was already there and waiting. She laughed that I had picked this up quickly. During one visit she also mentioned that two Spirit Guides, a male and a female were there with us. I could feel their energies on both sides of my head, and knew which one was male by the strength of his "buzzing."

In 2008 during a workshop with Dr. Weiss, he told the group to go back in utero, and I was thrilled. I heard my mom, Emily, and my dad, Al, talking. My dad wanted a boy – my sister was two-years-old – so it was understandable. My mom just wished it would be a healthy baby.

She was worried because she was taking dangerous fertility drugs and already had two miscarriages. I heard their voices so clearly and it was amazing and unmistakable. My Dad died in 1968, and after forty years I heard his voice again. It was undoubtedly him and I was very happy for this "reunion."

I've only had two contacts with my dad from 1991 to 2008. In the first, I believe that he entered into one of my dreams and told me that he liked my boys. That was all he said and he was gone in an instant.

In the second contact, during a meditation, I saw him in the distance standing among a sea of children in Heaven. There were only five adults surrounded by hundreds of children under five years of age. I must have asked my Angels if they knew where my dad was since he never "popped-into" my meditations. He did, however, make appearances in a very big way during my visits with Denver psychic medium Rebecca Rosen which are described elsewhere.

My mom died in 1990 but she had been visiting me in meditations for seventeen years at that point, but to hear her voice as a young woman worried about her unborn child was a gift. There were three other parts to this regression, and all I can recall is meeting with my Spirit Guide and Guardian Angels to discuss this experience and the conference.

Dr. Weiss's regression unleashed memories that were stored in my subconscious for fifty-five years, and the work he has done helping to heal people around the world is inspiring. His books are fascinating, and I recommend them if you are interested in learning about past lives in order to discover answers potentially to problems in your present life. And the good part is that, despite its name, a regression won't take you back down the rungs of your ladder as you discover your past lives. Instead, it will take you higher up the ladder of your spiritual journey. Think one step backward equals two steps forward.

Let's look back at what I experienced:

• A life in the mid-1800s in Kentucky, where two locations I visited in 1992 seemed familiar to me.

- A past life as a pioneer woman, with supporting evidence from my son's schoolwork.

- Scenes that explained reasons for my fear of heights, water, and nature.

- Scenes of lives and deaths in Mexico, Peru, and New Mexico, even though I have no affinity for these places or any reason to think, view, or relive these scenes.

- My murder as a Revolutionary War-period boy and scenes of him as a ghostly figure. In this life, I have a strong interest in this era of American History.

- I heard my parents' voices from a 1953 conversation.

Now aren't you the least bit interested in attempting to uncover your past lives? To discover the reasons behind your fears, talents, and relationships? Or why you prefer certain countries, cultures, or cuisines above others? Past life regressions are amazing and fun... if you are open to the experience. And you can do them alone, with the help of another, or in a large group where the concentration of spiritual energy is invaluable. While regressions are fascinating, I've always been more interested in what's coming up in my life and in receiving Divine Guidance from my Angels and Spirit Guides.

"Just look forward to your future. You will be blessed by the Hand of God. Trust us, your time is coming."

eleven

See Me, Feel Me, Hear Me, Know Me

Are you wondering how you, an average non-psychic person, can possibly receive information from Spirit, and what it seems like? If you aren't, you're reading the wrong book.

God, Angels, Guides, and Spirits are able to communicate with us through the four "clairs":

Clairvoyance is clear seeing. We are able to see clear images in our mind's eye or outside ourselves.

Clairsentience is clear feeling, where we suddenly feel or sense a divine message, or have a "gut feeling."

Clairaudience means clear hearing, where we are able to hear guidance or warnings, whether inside or outside our head.

Claircognizance means clear knowing, where we suddenly "just know" some information without knowing how we know.

On two occasions over breakfast, I grabbed the local newspaper and said aloud that our neighbors' photos were on the back page. I immediately separated the sections, turned the correct one over, and saw the neighbors and their family members in photos. I did this without any previous knowledge that these photos had been taken or submitted.

My clairvoyant experiences primarily focus on my ability to see Angels and Spirits in my mind's eye when I meditate. As I begin, I feel pressure on my third-eye chakra and know that it is opening to receive communication from the Other Side. Chakras are energy centers located in our body that control specific sections and functions. There are seven chakras and the third-eye chakra is associated with inner seeing, intuition, and higher consciousness. As I sit at the computer and type this sentence, I feel great pressure. I admit that at times I meditate and receive nothing at all. I believe it's because I've taken too long between meditations, and I'm out of practice. When I "arrive" and there are no Angels or Guides to greet me, I wait. And wait. And then wait some more, until I fall asleep. That is why I prefer to use a tape when I meditate. There is a timed ending that awakens me.

I have been admonished many times for meditating too often between attempts. *"Paul, we just spoke with you. What do you want now? What had time to change for you?"*

What they really mean is that they're busy and to leave them alone. They're in Heaven with plenty to do besides answer my questions repeatedly. Only they're far too polite to say that.

Here are a few clairvoyant examples from my past:

On Father's Day in 2000, I awoke at six a.m. and went out the front door to get the Sunday newspaper from the driveway. As I opened the front door, I once again asked my Angels for a sign that they were around me. I love doing this because I never know what will happen.

I opened the front door to a beautiful sunny, blue sky, and with my first step onto the porch, a flash of light in the distance caught my eye. I stopped and looked across the street. Between two homes I could see part of the Colorado National Monument called Flat Rocks, a number of smooth rock formations that slope upwards. It was at least twelve miles away. The curved formations resemble fairways on a golf course, and they are clearly visible throughout the Grand Valley.

A twinkling golden light appeared and then began to rise and grow, mesmerizing me. It rose straight up and then branched to the right and left as it continued to rise. When it finally stopped, it was a huge, glowing cross of gold. I was amazed. Who wouldn't be? It had to be at least two hundred feet tall and one hundred and fifty feet wide by my later estimates. I shook my head and remembered that, since it was Father's Day, a local church must have erected this majestic cross. There'd been a giant cross in the foothills southwest of Denver for decades, so why couldn't a Grand Junction church do it, as well?

I retrieved the newspaper, came back to the porch, and watched this magnificent sight for a few minutes. I wondered if I should wake Terry up to see it, too, but decided against it since it was only six a.m., and I'm not a stupid husband. Besides, she could see it for herself later, I thought.

I went back only minutes later, but it was gone. I thought they shut the power off, and I excitedly told Terry about the amazing cross I had seen. In fact, for the next two weeks I told everyone I came in contact with, but apparently no one else saw my Cross of Gold. They all looked at me as if I were crazy. When I meditated, my Angels and Guides laughed and said that I always asked them for a sign, yet when they gave me an unmistakable one, I doubted it. A psychic medium later confirmed what they said during a session. It was truly an unforgettable sight— apparently meant just for me to see.

I've had other fun experiences with lights. Maybe I should call them Angel Lights or Spirit Lights. I went to a Denver psychic in 1997, and we sat at a small café table in her reading room when I suddenly blurted out, "Do you see any Angels around me?" A second later, a golden ball of light appeared less than two feet to the left of my face and opened up. (Just a note: You can try it yourself. Make a fist with your left hand, and then open all of your fingers wide.) The star-like light twinkled, closed into itself, and disappeared. I looked over at the laughing psychic who said, "Yes, I do." I wasn't scared, but I froze and cringed just a little. I'll go out on a limb and say it wasn't a ball of lightning—it was an Angel. The psychic then told me of a television script sale with a bonus, and that happened a week later. She was over ninety-nine percent accurate on the dollar amount. I later spoke on her radio show, and my testimonial was used in her advertising.

In 2008, I was in our bedroom, and I looked up to see twelve tear-shaped, silver-and-copper-colored lights floating above me, just out of reach. They danced and twirled, doing figure eights, and I watched— amazed and entertained—for a few minutes until they just vanished.

Months later, while attending a "Celebrate Your Life" spirituality conference in Phoenix, I rode the hotel's steep escalator down to the morning sessions. I looked up to see an enormous tear-shaped sculpture hanging from the ceiling above me. It was identical in shape and color to the dozen lights I had seen at home. Had the Angels suggested that I go to the conference and then let me know that they were with me for support?

Then in 2013, we went to Scottsdale, outside Phoenix, for a quick vacation to see games of our beloved teams, the Colorado Rockies and Colorado Avalanche, and the lights returned!

I was in our hotel room and looked up to see ten lights swirling above me, just out of reach. They were the same metallic-liquid color, but in the shape of large M&Ms, not tear-shaped. Shouting excitedly that the lights were back, I called for Terry to run into the room and take a look. When she approached, I turned towards her, and when I looked back, they had disappeared.

Oh, darn, it was the Golden Cross all over again. But they sure were a treat to see. More like a gift. Actually, more like a little "hello" from my friends in Spirit.

Flashes of lights signify that Angels or Spirits are near, and I've had quite a few experiences seeing orbs drift by me and disappear into walls and closets. Psychics see flashing lights behind me and say that I have a huge team of Angels and Guides around me.

I was getting a book autographed by Dr. Doreen Virtue when she hesitated and looked up, and up, and up behind me. The ceiling was at least thirty feet high, and whatever stood behind me certainly caught her eye. She didn't tell me what she saw, but I later spoke with a woman who knew her well and was told that she does that when she sees Angels.

Psychic medium John Holland did the same thing as we checked in at a conference in 2008 and I was saying hello to an acquaintance. He bent far to the right from his waist and stared at me, then looked up, eyes wide. I wondered what he saw from the strange look on his face, but I didn't ask. My son, Joel, once saw a six-foot-tall flash of light behind me.

I've previously mentioned seeing Spirits when giving readings, and another just popped into my head. In 2012, I went over to a friend's home where she was recovering from surgery. I wanted to try a reading outside of a workshop setting. We sat on the living room sofa, and I began. When I closed my eyes, I could see, hovering above her, the outline of two men and two women, in pastel shades of blue and pink. The men—John and Frank—identified themselves as uncles, and one of the women said she was a friend from a past life when they were farmers in northern California in the late 1800s. The other female spirit didn't speak.

One of the men showed me images of himself on the floor in front of a Christmas tree as he gave horsey-back rides to my friend and her sisters. I had a hard time hearing what the two uncles said, and whenever I turned my head to the left, I clearly saw my Guardian Angels and Spirit Guide. They told me that I didn't prepare myself properly to give this reading so I struggled.

I get yelled at a lot by my Angels and Guides. Not exactly yelled at, but I sense their disapproval. Imagine four Spirits, hovering in front of you while trying to give you information that you aren't quite receiving, and, off to the left, there are two Angels and your Spirit Guide, shaking their heads.

My friend didn't feel any connection to the Spirit who was a very old friend, but I did get the names of the two uncles right, as well as the horsey-back rides at Christmas and one other identifying piece I can't read from my notes.

I took a test for psychic ability, in which five scenic images were shown and I had to select one. The correct image would then show up on the right side of the computer screen. I just relaxed my mind, and in my head I saw the correct answer.

I went ten for ten. Now when we go to Las Vegas, my wife likes to play the one-cent video slots, games like *Sex and the City* and *The Wizard of Oz*. When I stop by to check on her and she's winning, she lets me choose one of three "doors" concealing characters that lead to bigger winnings and bonus play. I stare at the "doors," then pick the winner enough times that ladies playing the next machines ask me to choose for them, as well.

I'm not a gambler, but the times that I've wanted to play roulette, I stand and watch for a bit. When I successfully pick either red or black for ten consecutive spins, I buy my chips, sit down to play, and immediately lose on every, single spin.

For years when I turned on the computer, there was a little image of an envelope signifying our e-mail. Before the number of e-mails would arrive onscreen, I stared at the envelope and called out the number I thought it would be. I was right fifty percent of the time. Not wonderful, but not bad.

In 1985, I was filling out a lottery card and saw six numbers associated with my ex-wife in my mind's eye. I penciled in the numbers but then decided not to play them. I tore up the card, went to the store, and bought Quick Picks instead. Can you guess what happened? I didn't win eight million dollars—four hundred thousand dollars a year for twenty years.

You don't have to be smart to be clairvoyant.

One morning I was getting ready for the day in our bathroom, when an image of a pretty blonde woman flashed into my mind. She had been a waitress at a local restaurant, and we always hoped she'd be our server when our family ate there. It seemed odd since we hadn't been there for at least five years, moved across the state, and didn't have any contact with—or knowledge of—her outside of the restaurant. I walked into our home office, and there she was, on NBC's *Today Show*, being interviewed from Vail, Colorado, on an animal rights issue. A year later, I was back in Denver and in line to buy a movie ticket. I looked around, and standing to my left was the same blonde woman. I thanked her for always being so nice to our family, and we both felt good, but I never mentioned the rest.

In March 2010, I went to Portland, Oregon, with my son Joel to spend a weekend with my older son, Chris, who hadn't been in touch for a while. Reviewing my meditation notes recently, I discovered that while meditating two days earlier, my Angels and Guides made sixteen correct statements regarding our visit. I wish I could access that kind of amazing guidance regularly, don't you?

Clairaudience means clear hearing, and occasionally Spirit creates words, sounds, or music internally in my head, and externally during warnings—and one loud-and-clear "quit-complaining" message I'll never forget.

Every once in a while I hear someone yell out, *"Paul,"* and look around to see no one at all. A few times it has been my mother, for sure. Those are just little "hellos" to let me know that someone is visiting.

I hear music in my head with the word, "Angel," in the title or lyrics. That's a given for over twenty years, mostly in the shower because I think the running water conducts their energy better and my brain isn't filled with "chatter."

A few years ago on a Florida vacation, my wife and I walked into a grocery store when I clearly heard Terry's Uncle Jay say "Buy Didie a Mother's Day card from Sarge." Uncle Jay died the year before, and Sarge was his dog that his daughter, Didie, inherited. I bought the card, and it was really appreciated—a nice, thoughtful sentiment from the Other Side.

Last winter, we received an e-mail from a good friend stating that her mother had just passed away. Terry sent an e-mail of condolence from her office, and then I sent one from our home. Afterwards I jumped into the shower, and immediately heard a woman shout, *"Tell her I'm alright!"*

I quickly looked around as if I expected to see someone there, but there wasn't anyone. Curious, I asked, "Who is this?"

"Frances. Tell her I'm alright!"

I looked around again. I don't know any Frances. Who's Frances?

Under the circumstances and the timing, I sent another e-mail to our friend and told her what just happened. I asked if either her Mother or Father (who passed years ago) were named Frances or Francis. I had never met her mother, who was always referred to as "my mom" or "Jane's mom," so asking such a delicate question just hours after her Mom's passing was a leap of faith.

I have an agreement with my Angels and Guides that I will pass along any information that they want me to—no matter how uncomfortable it is for me. Jane was having lunch with her family when she read my e-mail, and shared it with them. She wrote back that her mom's name was Frances, and she later told me that it made her family happy to receive that information. Jane, a very spiritual person herself, has shared my experiences with her family. She was the person whose two uncles came through in the reading I gave.

I told her that her mom had quite a morning. She got to go Home to Heaven and see me in the shower on the same day. The song lyric— "You've got to go through Hell before you get to Heaven"—must be true.

Writing about Jane's mom made me remember a visit from another mom. My neighbor's mother passed away at the age of ninety-seven. A year later, the neighbor dropped something off at our home. I was in the kitchen as she left and pulled the front door closed behind her, when I heard a voice yell out.

"Ask about her mom."

Whoa, I flinched big time, and blurted out "Have you heard from your mom?" just as the door shut. I regretted it instantly. The door never quite closed and the neighbor walked back in, and over, to me. She said the strangest thing happened a little while ago. Her mother's recipe for fried rice sat by itself in the center of a long kitchen counter, and she had no idea how it got there. Her mother's recipes were in a book on the top shelf in a cabinet across the kitchen, and she hadn't used it for a while. She's tiny and has to use a stepstool to even reach it, so getting her mother's recipes requires some effort. Lucky for me her mother gave her a little "hello" that morning since asking someone if they've heard from their deceased parent is not something anyone would be comfortable with.

But when Spirit yells something in my ear, or head, I tend to react quickly. Over the years, but primarily from 1999-2005, I have received shouted warnings from disembodied voices behind my left shoulder ten times while driving.

Ten, count 'em, ten.

I'd drive down the road and heard "Stop!" or "Look-out!" and quickly reacted by swerving or slamming on the brakes as other vehicles ran stop signs or red lights. I avoided getting hit and possible serious injury or car damage.

Ten times, I swear. You can't make this stuff up.

The most recent event was a new experience. After my accident in June, 2012, I was learning how to walk again and wore a protective boot and used a walker. I was down at the entrance to our neighborhood off a country road and looked in all directions before I attempted to cross. Hey, I wasn't the Captain of the Patrol Boys in eighth grade for nothing; I got skills. I saw no traffic, so I hobbled across the street. Halfway to the opposite curb, I heard a shouted warning.

"Watch out for the yellow car!"

What yellow car? I didn't see any yellow car when I left the safety of the curb at the stop sign on the corner. I quickly scanned the road, and rising out of a dip was a yellow car that I recognized was going to turn my way. I hustled across the street as fast as I could and made it onto the curb just as the yellow car made a right turn closer to me than I cared for.

As I typed the last sentence, a warning from our vacation in San Diego in 1996 popped-into my head. One night we left our hotel on Mission Bay and drove in search of Terry's beloved M&Ms. As we approached an intersection and I was about to turn left to go to a 7-Eleven, I heard a voice in my head say *"Don't go there!"*

Okay, whoever you are, I won't. I pulled out of the left lane and headed towards La Jolla, a few miles north, where we'd seen another 7-Eleven on our walk that afternoon.

On our way back with the M&Ms, when we reached the earlier intersection, I spotted two police cars with their lights flashing and realized that I had been warned to stay away. The store had been robbed at gun point, and we could have been there at the wrong time except that I heeded my warning.

I also hear loud warnings in regards to people familiar to me in my proximity that could be a potential problem or very uncomfortable situation. In those ten cases I clearly heard a voice inside my head or behind my left ear issue a warning.

"You're going to see (so-and-so). Look out. Don't react. Be careful."

And a few times the warnings were even stronger. In all cases, I turned in a store or parking lot to see the person in question approaching. One time the person was standing next to me, a mere three feet to my left, and I simply walked away. Another time I heard the warning as I rounded the corner on my hotel room floor and entered the area where the bank of elevators was. As I turned the corner, an elevator door opened and the person in question stepped out and edged past me. I believe that if my Angels warn me of a person's presence, they believe an unpleasant encounter could ensue, so I gladly heed their warnings. It has happened with pick-pockets and would-be muggers as well.

In the late 1990's I was playing first base in a slow-pitch softball game. A large left-handed slugger was at the plate and I played deep because this guy had crushed the ball in previous at-bats. Our pitcher released the ball in a high, slow arc and I got down in a crouch with my glove out front ready to field when I suddenly heard a voice say *"Watch your teeth."* I turned my head to the left towards the first base coach and umpire and said "What?" just as the hitter crushed the ball and sent a line drive screaming towards my face. I turned my head back just as the ball grazed my right earlobe, rocketed out into right field, and hit the fence three-hundred-and-fifteen feet from home plate after the second bounce. For you football fans, that's one-hundred-and-five yards on two bounces. That softball moved fast enough to destroy my teeth and possibly snap my neck as well. Fortunately, a disembodied voice warned me just in time to save me from a very serious accident.

I read in one of Dr. Doreen Virtue's books that Angels sound almost Shakespearean at times. They are to the point and blunt, something that Sylvia Brown writes in probably every one of her books when she mentions her Spirit Guide, Francine.

In my years of meditating and taking notes, I have to agree with both fine authors. My Guardian Angels speak to me in a loving, yet stilted, style, while my Spirit Guide, Dan, is a wise guy and comedian if we're alone. Otherwise he's on his best behavior around my Angels or higher-level Guides.

Your Higher Self, or your soul, sounds like your own voice, which I think is amazing as well. If for some reason, I doubt that I'm receiving messages from my Angels and Guides, at least I know that I'm not making up the information I receive – it's coming from my soul. I know I'm able to communicate with my soul because my conscious mind wouldn't ever think of, or have knowledge of, the things I hear during my meditations.

For instance, our son, Joel, put together a book of photographs and quoted me on one of the pages, only it wasn't me. He looked through one of my journals and liked this thought:

"Inner happiness is the fuel of success."

I never said that. Inner happiness? Fuel of success?

Me? No way.

Sorry, it was a message to me from my Angels or Guides, so I don't want to take any credit for it. It would be like holding someone else's Oscar, or lifting hockey's Stanley Cup if you didn't win it. I'm not going to do it.

Besides, taking credit for a Heavenly quote would no doubt have eternal ramifications—something I wouldn't want to risk.

We took a vacation this past April, and I went downstairs for the breakfast buffet. I was the only person in the room at the buffet table, yet as I walked into the seating area, I heard a woman shout, *"Tell me about it!"* At the coffee station, one other person was pouring herself a cup of coffee, and she paid no attention to me. She obviously hadn't shouted, yet the words had come from the direction of the coffee station. Confused, I walked over to an empty table—it was six a.m., so they were all empty—and sat down to eat my meal and read the paper. About thirty seconds later, a man and woman walked into the area, and the second woman said something to the first woman who suddenly yelled out, *"Tell me about it!"* Apparently I "heard" the first woman's response thirty seconds before she said it, loud and clear. That's new for me.

Claircognizance means clear thinking whereby Spirit places information into our minds from out-of-the-blue, and we have no idea where it comes from. From my many books on spirituality I've compiled some notes:

Claircognizants are intellectuals who receive direct communication through ideas and revelations and often know facts without having heard or read anything on the topic.

These folks are not comfortable with small talk, feel un-easy around other people, and prefer one-on-one conversations about subjects that interest them. They are seen as "know-it-alls" (ah, if only I had a dollar...). They generally have higher IQs and are avid readers with a wide range of interests.

They are skeptical about Angels and psychic abilities— unless they've had a dramatic lifesaving experience they can't explain. They know how things will turn out and are usually right, and they often have ideas about business or products that turn out to be correct. If they're searching for lost items, they ask Angels where they are and receive a sudden knowledge of the location of the items. I mention finding keys, hat and gloves, and my traveling tea bag in stories elsewhere.

From my own experiences, I have three stories to share.

Back in 1986 or 1987, there was a national scandal over a well-known preacher and his secretary. I wrote a letter-to-the editor to one of the Denver newspapers. It was playfully tongue-in-cheek and poked fun at the situation. I wrote it in the evening and planned to put it in the mail the next morning. Well, about two a.m. I awoke with a second letter running through my head. I got out of bed and began typing when I realized this was not my work at all—but a polite condemnation of the situation.

The next morning I showed it to a coworker, alongside my original one, and the tone and style were so different that there was absolutely no way it could have been written by the same person. And it wasn't. The second letter was written by Spirit, and I got to type it, mail it, and see it printed in the newspaper. Spirit had a finger-wagging message to share, and I was the vehicle used.

Another example of claircognizance occurred when I was searching our home for a great photo of Terry's mother, Ruby, and her Aunt Fran. Terry's cousin had just found a photo of the two of them, young and pretty, in 1940s-style dresses and hairstyles, and we had misplaced it.

I told Terry I'd look for it, and trust me, I did. I couldn't find it anywhere in the house. I was in the bedroom and asked my Angels for help, and suddenly I turned and stared at Ruby's desk that Terry had inherited. I walked over and flipped up a hand-crocheted doily that was draped over the front of the desk. Then I lifted the front edge—for no apparent reason—and discovered a secret drawer, front and center.

I had never used the desk or even touched it. Terry had her jewelry and things on top, and the drawers were tiny. I opened the drawer, and inside was the missing photo of Ruby and Aunt Fran. We were not sure if Terry had put it there and forgotten about it, or if my Angels did when I asked for their help. They had definitely impressed upon me the need to look somewhere I never would have thought of checking. Similarly, when I was renting a jackhammer, my head suddenly swiveled hard, and I spotted a pair of safety goggles. We had just built our new home and decided to add a deck, but the concrete step outside the breakfast nook needed to be removed. Can you guess what happened? I started the jackhammer, and within ten seconds a chunk of jagged concrete the size of my fist broke off, flew up, struck the right lens of my safety goggles, and jerked my head back. Had I not heeded the head-swiveling "message" to get the goggles, I could have easily lost my right eye.

One last claircognizance item: A couple of years ago while meditating, I was warned to check on land we owned because someone was trying to steal it. I did, and it turned out to be true.

Clairsentience means a clear feeling or sensing of Divine guidance where you have a strong gut feeling. I believe that my experiences with clairsentience overlap with those I've already mentioned with claircognizance, so I'll just mention some of the characteristics that seem to apply to me.

I'm a highly sensitive person and have difficulty in crowds. I feel an overload of energy and get nasty headaches and grow quiet. I am teased at times for being too sensitive, but that very sensitivity allows me to feel the presence of Angels and Spirits, and sometimes ghosts. During vacations we may walk into a historic building, and I just know that standing nearby is a presence staring at me. Later, reading a book, I discover that location, and sometimes that particular room, is haunted. I can tell—probably daily—if there are Spirits standing nearby as I suddenly turn and stare at a spot and request that they reveal themselves to me. I often feel someone touch my head or arms, and there are changes in air pressure or temperature around me. Upon meeting someone for the first time, I get an immediate reaction and know if I'm going to like this person or not, or I pick up on people's feelings if they're upset about something.

I quite often know when the telephone is about to ring and who is calling, or I get a feeling that someone is thinking, or speaking about me, at that moment.

At times I get a feeling of dread—or even fear—and I avoid certain situations and locations, such as the M&Ms/7-Eleven episode in San Diego, and my panic in two inches of river water, as well as a lifelong fear of being near armored cars.

I get feelings of excitement that something good or bad is happening at that moment to a loved one. Later I discover that my premonition and timing were perfect.

Mentally I call upon my Angels to surround and protect me whenever I feel uncomfortable in any situation—especially to surround and keep me upright as I go for walks on my healing leg, ankle, and feet. So far, so good.

I get strong feelings cautioning me not to do business with certain individuals or businesses, or even answer a telephone call. If it weren't for my contact with Angels, Spirit Guides, and Departed Loved Ones, I imagine being clairsentient wouldn't be any fun at all.

What about you? Has reading about my experiences with the four "clairs" released any memories of your own? Have you written them down in the margins? It's allowed, unless you're reading a library book, in which case you can expect to hear a loud, *"Don't do that!"* in your head—if you're lucky enough.

Or you can sit quietly for a moment, close your eyes, and clear your head of any chatter. Then ask Spirit to remind you of any past guidance that you have been allowed to see, feel, hear, or know. You can try to reestablish your connection to Heaven— the connection we all have available to us but have forgotten, or are afraid to use. Then trust the wisdom and guidance that comes forward.

But hold onto your ladder with both hands in case Spirit's response is unmistakable, the way it is when I ask for guidance using my Tarot cards.

twelve
Tarot Cards

After my spiritual journey began, I visited a psychic who used Tarot cards in her reading. I was curious to learn how the cards were utilized by Spirit to transmit messages to the reader, and I believed that I could use them to complement my meditations.

Tarot cards are used as a fortune-telling technique and consist of a deck of seventy-eight picture cards: twenty-two Major Arcana cards and fifty-six Minor Arcana cards. The Major Arcana cards deal with greater life events, and the Minor Arcana cover more mundane and everyday facets. Remember the word, "mundane," because it appears later.

I use my Tarot cards as a means of receiving guidance from my Angels and Guides. Solely for entertainment purposes, of course. I wanted to call this section, "Fun with Tarot Cards," so you could feel my excitement as I shared my experiences.

I use the most widely recognized Rider–Waite deck, and rely on Nancy Garen's *Tarot Made Easy,* which simplifies the process. You simply ask a question, and the book has answers for each card in thirty-two categories. If you want to know about Travel, Work/Career, Family, Finances, Success, Special Guidance, etc., etc., this book will give you concise predictions or guidance.

Since I was already in contact with my two Guardian Angels, David and Arianna, and my Spirit Guide, Sennodan(*"Call me Dan"*), I asked them to select cards from the deck that would identify them and let me know when they were present. I shuffled the deck of seventy-eight oversized cards loosely to allow for the cards to "fly out." This is so cool to see the way my Spirits do it.

Anyway, I can barely shuffle a regular deck of fifty-two cards. With seventy-eight cards, I have to spread my fingers wide and shuffle even more slowly and deliberately. Tarot cards are used as oracles and absorb the energy of their owner, so whenever I use them—maybe every ten days to two weeks—I sit at our dining room table and shuffle, cut, split into piles, and reshuffle over and over, as I ask my friends to come and give me guidance.

David selected the "Temperance" card for himself, meaning that as I shuffled, this card flew out of the deck with a flourish. It shot up and out of the deck about two feet above my head and landed straight and face-up on the table in front of me, as if looking right at me. This is how David continues to make his presence known to me. The Temperance card depicts an Angel in a white robe with extended wings and blond hair. I've never seen wings on David when I meditate, but he does have blond hair that cascades to his shoulders. He is very handsome and must be almost ten feet tall. He's very matter-of-fact when he "speaks" to me telepathically.

A quick aside: When I started this section, I absentmindedly opened the *Tarot Made Easy* book with its 383 pages and looked down to see the page with an image of the "Temperance" card looking back at me. In my experience, that means David is letting me know that he is here with me as I write this chapter.

Arianna selected the "Strength" card showing a white-robed female figure that closes the mouth of a lion. Above her head, she has the symbol for "Infinity," like a sideways figure eight. In my meditations, Arianna is also nearly ten feet tall and has long hair in sections of white, silver, and various shades of gray. She is very loving and tender, and she calms me when I'm upset, often calling me, "Dear Paul."

My Spirit Guide, Dan, selected "The Emperor" as his representative card, which shows a crown-wearing white-bearded man holding his scepter as he sits on a throne. Dan is quite the jokester so I'm not surprised he chose this regal-looking card. Seven psychics or psychic mediums in a row have seen him standing behind my right shoulder at readings, and one compared him to John Travolta's mobster character, Chili Palmer, in the film, *Get Shorty*.

I don't use the cards in spreads like the three-card or the Celtic Cross. When I use the Tarot cards, I shuffle them loosely and ask my friends to show themselves to me. What I'm really asking them to do is materialize—preferably across the room so I don't get frightened—but they never do. Instead, their cards fly out and land before me neatly and facing up. I laugh because it's amazing to see, and it seems as if my Angels and Spirit Guide stand right next to me, reach in, and pull out the cards as I shuffle.

It works another way, as well. When I shuffle the cards and I clearly hear them in my head say *"Cut"* or *"Look,"* I immediately stop shuffling and randomly cut the cards, or I flip the deck over to reveal the Temperance, Strength, or The Emperor cards. I then lay the card on the table and ask a question, like "What do you want me to know about...?" Before I can finish the sentence, another card flies out and lands on top of the first card, or at least makes contact with it. Other cards simply "fall out" as I shuffle, and after twenty years I know the difference by the feel of it.

This is how David, Arianna, and Dan communicate with me. Most of the time the "answer card" will fly out before I finish my question, as if they already know what I'm about to ask. I then use the book to look up what they want me to know at that time.

For years I started my sessions by holding the Tarot book by its spine so the side of the pages faced up. I'd slowly pass my right hand over the top of the pages and lower it slightly until I felt the energy of the book, and then the energy of a single page. I'd open the book to that page—let's say The Four of Swords—and I'd see the image of a knight in effigy upon his tomb with his hands in prayer and with three swords hanging above him and one on the side of his tomb. Then I'd ask my questions when David, Arianna, and Dan arrived, hopefully followed by the right cards and guidance. When I felt it was time to finish the session, I'd ask my Angels and Guides if they were really with me, and The Four of Swords would fly out of the deck onto the table or desk.

"Yes, we are here, and you are finished for today." This is how I took the message. So I started each session by feeling and selecting the energy of one of seventy-eight cards, and when I asked for proof, that card would make itself known. I did this for years and years and just stopped in the last few. I always asked for confirmation, and Terry said that I was insulting them, as if I didn't believe despite all I'd experienced.

I once asked my Angels and Spirit Guide that, if they were with me, could they make specific cards fly out of the deck as I shuffled. I'm seeing this in my mind's eye in our home office loft in the spring of 1999, as I type.

I asked for the Ace of Swords(my family crest)to appear from the deck of seventy-eight, and it did. And then the Ace of Cups, and it did, followed by the Ace of Wands, yep, and finally the Ace of Pentacles, yessiree. Can I get an Amen? I requested four specific cards in a row and got them. I believe the odds of that happening are thirty-six million to one.

Here's what's even cooler about it. As I started shuffling and asked for the first card, I heard Dan say, *"We don't do tricks."* OK, fine. Let's call it a demonstration of your abilities as an awesome Spirit Guide, because it certainly happened after he said it. How about a big round of applause for my Spirit Guide, Dan, folks—he'll be here all my life.

My birthday is on the twelfth, and the corresponding card is The Hanged Man. I believe this allows me to receive guidance from my Higher Self, or soul. When this card comes out in a session, I think there's something I need to hear to keep me on path, and then another card comes out with the information.

A few years ago I used the cards at my desk in our office. It's actually a long, glass dining room table because I don't like having my legs confined by drawers. As I shuffled, one card shot out of the bottom of the deck with great force and landed face up to my left. Now, the cards representing my Angels and Dan were on the table in front of me, so if this card was their message, it should have flown up a few feet and landed touching one of them, right?

Hey, I don't make the rules. I just follow them.

I picked it up, placed it back in the deck, and reshuffled. Four times in a row, this same card shot out from the bottom of the deck to my left. I asked aloud if that card was their message as I reshuffled because, if it was, why didn't it land on one of their cards?

In an instant the same card(let's call it the Sun card which has flashed in my mind's eye)shot out of the deck for the fifth time in a row! I looked at it and started to laugh, and then the Sun card stood up and walked itself over—left, right, left, right—about two feet to one of the Angel cards and slammed itself down on top of it.

This is my life; I kid you not. An invisible Spiritual Being manipulates these Tarot cards inches away from me, and I don't see it. Talk about being frustrated—but they're frustrated with me, as well—so I'll put words in their mouths and try to explain.

"Paul, we sent you the answer card five times in a row and you still don't believe it. If we make it stand and walk over so it lands exactly where you think it should, will you be happy then?"

Maybe.

Please note that in that exchange there was no *"Dear Paul"* included. Over the years they have discussed my impatience numerous times, and I know when I have overstepped more than a little bit.

A few years ago I was explaining my use of the Tarot cards to Joel during one of his visits. This was the very first time I used the cards in front of anyone. Joel sat snug against the armrest of our L-shaped sofa—my usual spot. I stood in front of the fireplace, eight feet from the end of the sofa's arm. I explained how my Angels and Spirit Guide used the cards, and they put on quite a demonstration for Joel.

I shuffled the deck as I spoke and the Temperance, Strength, and the Emperor cards revealed themselves fifteen times in a row. I demonstrated the "cut" and "look" techniques, and it was so impressive that sometimes those cards flew out and landed face up on the arm of the sofa, next to Joel, and they didn't fall off. He was more than a little freaked out.

Think about it—the same three cards in a deck of seventy-eight revealed themselves fifteen times in a row. Break it down to a one-in-twenty-six chance or 3.85 percent. To the fifteenth power!

And that's just the math!

What about the physics? From eight feet away, how do you get the cards to fly out and land face up on the arm of a sofa without falling off? I believe the cards landed safely on the arm eight out of fifteen times. You can try it yourself. Get two decks of playing cards and from one of the decks remove the suits of clubs and spades. Add them to the other deck, which now has seventy-eight cards—fifty-two black and twenty-six red. Shuffle the cards repeatedly, and make the Jack, Queen, and King of Hearts reveal themselves fifteen times in a row using my "cut," "look," and "jump-out" techniques.

Oh yeah, don't forget to get them to fly out face up and land on the arm of a piece of furniture, as well.

Since playing cards are smaller than Tarot cards, this should be easier, right? Go ahead and try, and you'll realize it's not a trick. It's an amazing demonstration by Spirit.

In July 2013, Spirit started something new. As I shuffled and asked them by name, if they were with me, their corresponding cards would fly out, reverse themselves, and fly back into the deck, barely held in place by the very bottom of their card and fanned out so their images faced me as I stopped shuffling. It was amazing to see.

One afternoon David's Temperance card came out first the old-fashioned way. I started shuffling and asked out loud if Arianna and Dan were here, as well. Guess what happened?

By now, you should know what happened.

Both cards—Strength and the Emperor—flew out, reversed, and flew back in, facing me, as if saying, *"Ta-daaaaaa! Here we are, Paul."* Seriously, you can't make this stuff up because how could you even conceive it, much less execute it?

Recently I took my Tarot cards to Denver on their first road trip, and I shuffled absentmindedly infusing my energy into the deck, while I explained their new method of arrival to Joel. As I did, the Chariot card, which is associated with Joel's birth date and his Higher Self, flew out, reversed itself, and then came back into the deck by sticking out from an edge as a demonstration for Joel to see.

Remember when I said that I'd get back to the word "mundane"? I saw a Denver psychic, and when an Angel light appeared next to my head, my Angels gave her a message, in which they used the word "mundane." She said that was a strange word to hear, but not for me.

It falls under the "Special Guidance" category in my Tarot book, which has two separate answers for "mundane" and "esoteric." Because of my experience with the Tarot cards and the book, "mundane" was like a buzzword since I'm always asking for special guidance. The Angels asked the psychic to repeat it to confirm that they were indeed present in case the golden light that opened and closed next to my head wasn't enough to convince me.

Recently I did the cards at the dining room table, and hours later I was on the kitchen phone with my wife. As we spoke, I spotted a Tarot card on the floor in the dining room. As I approached it, I suddenly knew that it was The High Priestess card, the number two card of the Major Arcana. Terry's birthday is on the second, so I associate this card with her. I picked it up, turned it over, and it indeed was The High Priestess. Did I walk past this card lying on the carpet for four hours without noticing it, or did it appear from the office closet as I was speaking to Terry as another little "hello?"

I use Tarot Cards as another method of communicating with Spirit when I have questions about life. At times I use them right after I meditate to see if my Angels and Guides are "still around," as sort of a test. In any case, I find the cards entertaining since I am absolutely convinced that Spirit is with me at that moment, and I receive just enough guidance to let me know I am never alone. If you have any interest in seeing what type of communication you may receive via Tarot cards, I suggest you give it a try.

There was another time when I was absolutely convinced that Spirit was around me—when I was about to die a second time. I called upon my Angels for help, and my life was saved by a Second Miracle.

thirteen

The Second Miracle

Ten years after The Miracle in the River, I found myself in desperate need of a life-saving intervention again. You'd think I would have learned not to put myself in these situations; however, I was about to die until Spirit arrived.

One morning in April 2000, I meditated and made contact with my Angels. I don't recall any details of the session, but I will never forget what occurred five minutes later.

After meditating in the family room, I went into our home office to check e-mails and read the news. On the desk I saw a four-inch white feather, one that been plucked earlier from my infamous black velour pillow that for seven years seemed to have a never-ending supply of pluck-worthy feathers.

I absentmindedly picked up the feather and stuck the quill in my mouth, leaving the rest hanging from my lips—like a cool dude with a toothpick.

Big mistake. Really big mistake.

Something I read online initiated a reaction, and I inhaled quick and deep, swallowing the feather—all four inches!

I began to choke, and then to panic. Panic and choke. Choke and panic. The order didn't matter. The feather was lodged deep in my throat, and I knew that I was in real trouble.

I ran across the hall to the bathroom and leaned over the sink. I tried to dislodge the feather without success.

I looked up at my reflection in the mirror. My face was a deep red and darkening by the second to shades I'd never thought possible. My face was no more than a foot from the mirror, and I could see the terror in my eyes.

Terry was at work so I was home alone, and the realization that I was about to choke to death hit me hard.

I tried again and again to get that darn feather out. Glancing in the mirror once more, I saw my eyes and cheeks bulged out, and my head felt like it was about to explode as I continued to struggle and choke.

"Angels, help me!" I heard the words screaming inside my head. I had said good-bye to them only five minutes earlier at the end of my meditation, and I hoped that they would still be near.

Seconds later, golden flashes of light reflecting in the mirror caught my attention. Still leaning over the sink, I half-turned to my left and saw the golden lights begin to materialize no more than three feet away.

As more and more arrived, these twinkling flashes of gold began to take shape and rise, growing to twelve feet from floor to ceiling and filling a shaft that led to a sun tube on the roof.

The lights swirled around in revolving flashes that took the shape of a DNA Double Helix, a symbol for Life. I stood and stared at this unbelievable sight as I was still struggling for air.

What is it? How could it be possible? I turned back to the sink, tried to force the feather out, and then it happened again. A miniature DNA Double Helix of golden lights appeared no more than six inches away, right in front of my face. A foot tall and rotating, it was between me and the mirror.

I was stunned and probably in shock, as I turned toward the twelve-foot golden helix and then back to the one-footer, and then back again. I did this a few times, staring at them in awe as they rotated in unison.

Suddenly, I stopped choking and struggling for oxygen. I glanced at my reflection in the mirror and saw that my face was less red, and my cheeks were shrinking in size. I looked in the sink, but there was no feather there. I didn't swallow it because that would have been impossible to miss.

The feather just disappeared in my throat. As the swirling DNA Double Helices captured my attention, my Angels must have removed the feather. How else can I explain it? This was the second time I knew my death was mere seconds away, and the second time I was spared by the Grace of God. Believe me, when you realize that you are about to die, you become very focused on what you must do to survive. In 1990, I needed to break the surface of the water in the river with my hand and hoped my wife could rescue me. In 2000, I needed to dislodge a large feather from my throat.

In both cases, I failed. My efforts were not enough, no matter how hard I tried, and in both cases I asked God and His Angels for help.

And they replied with Miracles that saved my life on both occasions. Of this, I have no doubt—none at all.

In twenty-three years, I have told thirty-five individuals of these two Miracles. The more spiritual ones all say the same thing, verbatim:

"God has plans for you."

I certainly hope so, and I pray it is the work I've been doing during my meditations and "school" sessions all these years. Like the old saying goes: You know how to make God laugh? Tell Him your plans.

For the record, according to Wikipedia, Deoxyribonucleic Acid is a molecule that encodes the genetic instructions used in the development and functioning of all known living organisms... most DNA molecules are double-stranded helices... DNA, RNA, and proteins compose the three major macromolecules essential for all known forms of life.

To me, the DNA Double Helix is the symbol for Life. How fitting was it that two golden helices appeared when I cried out to my Angels for help?

I have shared these two Miracles and some of my other experiences at spiritual conferences and workshops with like-minded strangers—ones who seemed more apt to be accepting of these sort of stories. After all, if they weren't on their own spiritual paths, they wouldn't be looking for answers, would they?

As far as family, friends, and health professionals go, the number is only thirty-five in twenty-three years, and usually I tell them that there must be a message for them somewhere in what I share. Otherwise, I'm inclined to keep my experiences quiet. As I've read in so many spiritual books, people with similar experiences don't want to be ridiculed so they keep them to themselves. After all, who actually wants to be ridiculed?

However, we all know what has happened to us, and we usually have no proof or witnesses, and certainly not the knowledge and energy to explain and then defend ourselves to everyone. So I have an open mind when I read books where people share their experiences of visiting Heaven, being rescued by Angels, or saved by Miracles.

Look at how our society celebrates victims of crime and abuse or those battling addictions when they step forward to tell their personal stories. Yet people who have visits from their Departed Loved Ones or encounters with Angels "keep it quiet" to avoid ridicule.

Watch any talk show or morning news show where a celebrity guest announces that they haven't had a drink or a cigarette for three months, and the audience, crew, and hosts burst into applause. Better yet, they overcame an addiction—like all the female celebrities and ex-athletes who lose dozens of pounds of weight in a few months on a diet plan for a mere half-million dollars. Oh, my goodness, they're all over the television.

Now watch a psychic medium guest on the same television shows, and he/she is treated with skepticism and sometimes outright contempt. Excuse me, but I'll jump off my soapbox after a final comment.

Miracles happen. Deal with it.

Five months later, in a span of forty hours, I received two special visits from my Angels and Guides. This time they didn't need to perform a miracle, but they were on hand, just in case.

"You will be protected in this endeavor by God's Angels. Keep thinking of the work you are here to do and all will be well. You have survived this life to reach this point, and you will."

fourteen

My Heart Attack

⌒

August 29, 2000, was a Thursday morning, and Terry and I were packing for our weekend at the Aspen Jazz Festival. I leaned against the dresser and flipped through a recent Land's End catalog when I felt a sharp pain in my chest. I rose and felt more sharp pains, and then I spun around, convinced someone was stabbing me.

Of course, no one was there. I collapsed onto the bed, and then began to vomit clear liquid. I told Terry that I felt awful, walked to the kitchen, and drank some water. On my way back to the bedroom, I experienced a sharp pain in my left arm and realized that I was having a heart attack. Terry drove us the mile and a half to the regional hospital where she worked.

I told them that I just had a heart attack, and I was rushed into the ER. A cardiologist came in, was briefed by the nurse, and after hearing my family health history, he said, "You have absolutely no chance at all."

Not what I wanted to hear, Dr. Poker Face.

I was rushed into surgery thirty minutes after my first sharp pain. I tried to escape the heavy pressure on my chest by meditating. It felt as if my heart was being crushed in a Panini press. The two cardiologists prepared to enter through my groin and yelled at me to stay awake as I replayed my meditation tape in my head. As I went deeper, deeper, and deeper into my subconscious, the pain lessened more and more. My eyes were closed but in my Mind's Eye I saw that the walls of the circular room were now lined with Angels and Spirit Guides that I had met over the previous eight years.

Some nodded and smiled at me, others gave me a silent "thumbs-up," and I realized that I was going to survive. I relaxed and endured the procedure as a stent was inserted. When I reviewed my notes from a 2001 telephone session with Houston psychic medium Kim O'Neill, I saw that my Angels and Guides told her that they did not want to distract, or scare, the doctors. Had they spoken to me, I would have answered them aloud and would have died. I did tell one of the doctors what happened in 2012, twelve years after the event. Kim was told that he was a very spiritual man, and he accepted what I said.

I later spent three years in a study with our insurance company. They'd call and send questionnaires that asked why I was still alive since I had a very serious heart attack. I would be cute and say, "I guess God doesn't want me yet." Well, maybe not too cute since this was the third time He "threw me back," in addition to many shouted warnings, so I do have some experience staying alive.

I remember being wheeled out of the operating theater into the hallway on my way to Intensive Care. Terry was being briefed by one of the cardiologists, and I saw her, smiled, and gave her a thumbs-up to let her know I was going to be fine.

My first night was uneventful. I had to lie perfectly still on my back because my groin and artery were still "open," and that was tough because I like to sleep on my side. I felt very weak and drained, but I managed to tell Terry that my friends in Spirit came to reassure me, and that comforted her as well.

The next afternoon I was transferred to a regular room where I spent most of the day napping and praying I wouldn't have to use the bedpan. I never did, and never have, during that or the next five visits for heart procedures. Want to know my secret?

Prayer.

You can open my groin and send your cameras and instruments up inside my heart all you want. I don't care that it takes two men to break through the scar tissue, or that I can hear and feel the crunching despite the pain medication, but if you expect me to maneuver myself onto a bedpan and use it, we're going to dance, Mister. Actually, I'm going to lie helplessly weak in bed, but I'm going to have my wife give you a piece of her mind—provided she agrees with me.

I went to sleep that night with the window blinds open. There was a full moon hanging very low in the sky above the canyon walls of the Colorado National Monument. It appeared very close, like a grapefruit held at arm's length. My room was lit by the moonlight, as bright as if it were dusk. I slept on my left side and faced the doorway with the window to my back—no more than four feet from the bed.

At three a.m. my eyes sprung open. I was immediately wide-awake, glanced at the clock on the wall across from the bed, and suddenly sat straight up. My head swung from the clock over to the far corner of the window where I saw him.

An Angel stood leaning against the wall with his head tilted down and to the left so he could see the moon. He was huge. His eyes were at the very top of the window as he gazed out with a very peaceful expression. He was very handsome, with cascading golden hair that dropped down over his shoulders in aspen leaf-shaped locks. He had an aquiline nose and massive forearms folded across his chest. He wore a light-colored, short-sleeved robe in some pale shade of blue, green, or gray, but I saw no wings. I never see wings when I see my Angels unless they're on Angel Clouds.

He paid absolutely no attention to me and was completely focused on the full moon. I stared hard for fifteen to twenty seconds—which seemed like minutes under the circumstances. Then I did what I usually do when I see something from the Other Side. I covered my eyes with both hands and shook my head in disbelief. When I lowered my hands and peeked out, he was gone. I had broken the connection.

Still, I saw an Angel standing only eight feet away while wide-awake. If you've been a parent with a newborn baby and you awaken with a jolt and are immediately alert, you know what I mean. For my next few heart procedures, I'd wake up on the hour and half hour every night with the hope of catching another look at this Heavenly Being. His size and beauty were amazing, and to witness it up close was truly a gift. I went back later and measured. With his body leaning left against the wall and his head tilted, his eye level would have been eight feet above the floor.

I reviewed my 2001 telephone session notes, and psychic medium Kim O'Neill relayed that the Angel I saw was actually Dan, my Spirit Guide. He said that I had asked to see the Angels and Guides from the operating theater again. I was awakened at exactly 3 a.m. for that purpose—to provide proof that what I had seen forty hours earlier was real.

I say it was an Angel, but if it was my Spirit Guide, appearing in a different form than usual, I really don't care. I have never forgotten this amazing and beautiful sight, and I hope that I never will.

fifteen

Conference Readings

―

"It is never about you. Remember that."

A Second Miracle saves my life, and it's followed by a serious heart attack where I am comforted and watched over by Angels and Guides. Can you understand why I kept climbing the rungs of the ladder on my spiritual journey? There were so many wondrous things I had seen and learned, and I needed to discover where all of it was leading me. If I could see my Angels and Guides, I wondered if I could see anyone else's.

At some of the conferences and workshops I attended, speakers and authors have participants pair off and attempt to give readings to each another. You basically still your mind and allow Spirit to come through to you with information to pass along to your partner. I cover some of my experiences here and again in the section on Psychometry.

In a 2008 session in Phoenix with psychic medium and author James Van Praagh, I was paired with a very nice woman in her mid-sixties. As I focused, I saw a shadow box. Two-thirds of it contained a charcoal drawing of an older man's face, and the other third had a stylized number thirty-eight that reminded me of the numbers worn by the Atlanta Hawks of the NBA. The man's face was alive. He was laughing, talking, and very excited and happy—and I was shocked to say the least. In my Mind's Eye, I'm looking at a talking head in a box. He sent messages of love and his well-being, etc. My partner was very happy to hear from her late husband, and said their thirty-eighth anniversary was the next day. In my excitement, I never asked if she had a charcoal drawing of him or if he was a graphic designer. That still bothers me.

His energy pulled away, and our connection ended. I thought I was finished and was very surprised when a second man in Spirit came through. He was also very excited and appeared as a large dark shadow. I could make out his head, neck, shoulders, and upper torso as he stood behind the woman's right shoulder. His words flowed down a large, thick, dark blue arrow that passed between us, and I read them as fast as I could.

"Tell her that I always knew about her. I always loved her. I always saw her. I was always there, watching. I saw everything she did. Tell her that I love her." And then he disappeared.

"Did that make any sense?" I asked, sheepish. When I do a reading, I feel that it's my duty to pass along whatever I see and hear, and sometimes the speed is so great I can barely keep up.

She started to cry and smile. She told me that she knew exactly what the message meant. Once everyone involved in her life had passed, she looked into the circumstances of her birth and found out that she was an illegitimate child from a small town. She had always suspected this man was her father. Now in her sixties, she finally researched it and found out that she was correct.

It was a very good experience for both of us. On her first attempt to look into the possibility of life after death and communication with Spirit, both her husband and birth father paid her a visit. She was a nice lady, and I'm sure she had a wonderful and unexpected anniversary present.

At another conference in Scottsdale years before, I gave a reading to a woman from the state of Washington, and a dark, shadowy outline of a man came through. He said that he was her ex-husband and had died in a car accident. He wanted me to tell her that he loved her and always had.

This Spirit was intense, and his words flashed before me like a ticker tape. I spoke as fast as I could. I looked at the woman, and her jaw dropped as she stared at me.

When we finished, we returned to our seats, and it happened that she and a friend, a psychic, sat in the row behind me to my right. As she told her friend about my reading, the shadowy presence of her ex-husband suddenly appeared two feet in front of me. I cringed and froze, trapped. What could I do? Where could I go? He leaned in and said, *"You forgot to tell her I'm alright,"* and then he disappeared. I immediately turned around and told her that he just followed me back to my seat, and I gave her the rest of his message. I didn't care for having a large, intense Shadow Man follow and sneak up on me. It's the reason I rarely do this.

I later partnered with this woman's psychic friend, and we transmitted thoughts of images on postcards back and forth successfully. The women called out to James Van Praagh on stage and pointed at me. "This guy's good." He walked away. Yeah, whatever.

At the most recent conference we attended, Terry and I sat in author Denise Linn's workshop circle of eight attendees, and we took turns focusing on one person while we attempted to see that person in a past life. This was different and great fun.

I saw my wife, Terry, as a Roman slave in a palatial setting. She was a highly regarded teacher, and the children in her care loved her. They ran to give her hugs as the morning lessons began. With Terry's love of knowledge, education, and reading, it seemed so accurate, so real, so absolutely right.

I saw another woman as a medieval English princess, the youngest of three girls. They wore long blue dresses and those tall, pointy hats with scarves attached. They laughed and played on the walkways of the castle walls, and they tried to talk to their father. He was deep in conversation with two soldiers and had no time for the girls. The woman was thrilled to hear my thoughts, and they seemed to have a lot of meaning to her.

I saw another woman as a Native American in southwest Arizona hundreds of years ago. She was with a group of women, and they all talked and laughed as they prepared food by grinding corn in bowls. When I told her what I saw, she also was excited because this had a special meaning for her, as well.

And now to Mrs. Grumpy-Pants. There was a matronly woman in our group, and I saw her as a female entertainer of some renown in

San Francisco in the 1880s or 1890s. The city's high society all came to a theater to see her perform. She was young, beautiful, and talented, and Mrs. G-P wanted none of it. If looks could kill... I tried to explain that she was not a saloon girl or a prostitute, but a famous performer. Apparently that wasn't good enough for her. Actually, I threw in the prostitute part because I knew I had no chance of changing her mind, and her glare was uncalled for.

That was a good, fun experience for the one hundred or so folks in the session. The group's energy enabled most of us to pick up on possible past lives that seemed to have some relevance to the recipient. Well, almost. One lady told me that she saw me as a reptilian commander of a spaceship in another galaxy. Apparently I was a good guy—as reptilian space commanders go—so at least I had that going for me in a past life far, far away.

I enjoy attending conferences where I can meet hundreds of like-minded individuals interested in spirituality and hear my favorite authors speak and demonstrate their knowledge, psychic abilities, and talents. The energy there revitalizes me, and I believe the abundance of spiritual energy enables regular people like us to experience communication with Spirit. There's nothing like meeting total strangers and spouting forth the secrets of their lives while subtly leaning away from their imposing, excited, Departed Loved Ones.

My point is that you too can do it, along with the hundreds of others who attend these sessions and make the effort. You truly can, and you don't have to believe in it at all. Spirit will help you.

All it takes are two steps:

1. You have to come.

2. You have to try.

But these only count as one more rung up your ladder.

sixteen

The Council

⌒

*"Your unhappiness is due to your desire to fulfill
your Destiny and Sacred Contract. It is your Dark Night
that you have patiently gone through."*

Many times over the years I've complained to my Guardian Angels and Guides about the choices I made in my Contract—that they are seemingly impossible to fulfill. I have asked for their help in changing the goals I chose for this lifetime, primarily to release me from the promise I made to God while drowning.

Basically, I wanted out. This life was just too hard. Other people had easier, happier, and successful lives. Why couldn't I? It was whining at the highest level(someone just put that sentence into my head), and during meditations I often confronted my Angels and Guides to help me by petitioning the Council of Elders on my behalf, so that I might change the course of my life.

On two occasions that I remembered, I had been escorted to a large chamber with a huge U-shaped table. The chamber seemed dimly lit, but that was probably because of the strength of my "connection" during that meditation session.

I stood in the middle of the room and was flanked by seated Elders or Council Members. These men and women in their white robes and gowns seemed very old and very wise. My two Guardian

Angels and Spirit Guide stood at the opening of the table, and spoke on my behalf.

(NOTE: Someone behind my left ear just said, *"Stop whining."* I'm not. I'm merely sharing this experience about my whining.)

They "spoke" on my behalf, but I wasn't allowed to hear any of it. I could only hear if I was addressed directly. I stood, overwhelmed, and took it all in, like a tourist in a great museum—which I was. These were very impressive Spiritual Beings and somehow I was in their presence, not because of anything that I'd done, but because of my Angels' and Spirit Guide's love and compassion.

During one of my two visits, a young man stepped in front of me. He was wearing a white robe and had long, brown hair and a beard. He began to communicate, but I couldn't hear a word he said. When this occurred I expected that my subconscious would receive and understand the message, which would be useful in the future. From three feet away, he stood face-to-face with me, and I thought, "Gee, he looks like Jesus Christ," but even I found that hard to believe. I certainly didn't feel worthy of it.

I usually write without any religious references or symbolism, whenever possible. Not that I have any problems with that; it's just that I feel my experiences shouldn't shape your response to them by including overt religious symbolism. I believe I have visited Heaven, but since I have never seen the Pearly Gates or met St. Peter, I don't want to try to meet your expectations of it by embellishing anything.

It was a brief exchange with this calm, handsome man. He ended it with a warm smile and nod, and then he vanished. Soon afterwards, I was whisked away from the chamber and met with my "Team" in a small meeting room. When I asked what was said, I received a simple answer: *"They're discussing it."* Case closed. Move on, Paul. It was the Angelic equivalent of every parent's response when they reluctantly say the dreaded "We'll see."

Over my twenty years of being escorted during these meditations, I feel that since I haven't died—or wasn't in the midst of a near-death experience—that what I see and hear is somehow diminished. I don't see the most brilliant colors or hear wondrous Angel Choirs in song, or see cities of majestic beauty, or witness the throes of Angels. I get bits and pieces and visit specific locations. I always say that I can only see what I am shown—and nothing more. Everything I see is a gift, and I acknowledge and accept it as such, with gratitude and humility. This is why I have waited so long to write about my journey.

Here are some quotes from my meditation notes regarding my first visit with the Council of Elders:

They go over my chart, speak amongst themselves. *"You have learned patience, understanding, and compassion. You will never treat others the way you perceive yourself being treated. This will be necessary as you progress further with your destiny.*

"Everything is as you and we have preordained in your Chart. Continue to meditate, and learn more here in Heaven, for you are one of the truly spiritual souls who seek wisdom and truth in your existence. We will continue to monitor your progress and help you reach your destiny. Thank you for joining us today. Now go and seek further guidance from your Guide. Go in God's Peace and Love, and have faith. You will do God's work in His time."

I'm whisked away and find myself in the Spirit Guides' Temple in a pod-like office with Dan. He hugs me and smiles.

"See? Wasn't that wonderful? We are on path, no matter how unhappy or frustrated you get. This is where you need to be. By choosing to come here, your spirituality has made a dramatic increase. You leaped towards (your mission). I can't show you your Chart, but please know that we are working closely on your behalf. Relax and prepare. You can feel the energy of the temple and with the Council."

Now we meet with my Guardian Angels, David and Arianna, outdoors in a meadow filled with yellow flowers. We hug.

"We are proud of you for taking that next step in faith and spirituality. Continue on this path, Dear Paul. Continue to receive messages regarding (your mission) for these are events that will take place, and you are being shown them in order that you may know what to expect and how to behave. You will be very pleased to see these events in the near future."

They deliver personal family messages, and then David says, *"Continue with the guided meditations. Can you not see the difference in our contact? Continue to fear not and press forward. Your work is about to change dramatically."*

There is another personal message, and then David continues. *"Yes, this is your best visit ever. Now it is time to go. Continue your work."*

I open my eyes, and I'm back in my body on the recliner, groggy and happy after my best visit ever.

And in my second visit with the Elders regarding my Chart:

I asked if I was on course. *"Yes, your path is a very difficult one, but you must wait for the proper time as chosen by God. Be patient, Dear Paul, and try and see the benefit you have gained by going through the things that have stopped your life. You do all this for the glory of God."*

They offered details on my mission and added, *"Your soul is able to communicate freely with us. Your meditations are quite easy for you. Contact is no problem. Be aware that, once you begin, you will live your life on high speed, and there will never seem to be enough hours in the day."*

They provided more personal information before continuing: *"Your soul is softened and ready to accept the responsibility of God's work. You will accomplish much and change many lives. This is the path you have chosen and you are directly in it. Be proud. Now you will leave us. Go in God's Peace and Love. We will be watching and guiding your efforts. Go now!"*

The solemnness and importance of these meetings were overpowering. I wouldn't say I was frightened, but I was certainly intimidated.

One day I was very upset about my Chart and the difficulties I had chosen for this life. I meditated and begged God to let me out of my choices. I found myself whisked away to a place I had never seen before. I rose up and floated in a dimly-lit tunnel of grays, blues, and greens. It was enormous, and in the sides of the tunnel I could make out the shapes of Angels as they pressed against them, as if they came forward to make themselves known to me.

I rose higher and higher, and for the first time in any meditation, I was seriously frightened. This was so different and more intense than anything I'd experienced before. I felt that I didn't belong there, and I didn't want to stay any longer. Overcome with emotion, I cried uncontrollably. Spirit was communicating with me and I knew I was receiving information as I begged for my life to be changed. This experience was unlike anything else on my spiritual journey, and I was totally overwhelmed. I believe that I passed out and awoke hours later from that meditation session.

Even as I recall it now, I have an uneasy feeling that I wasn't supposed to see what I did.

Normally I say that I am like a toddler on the Other Side. I am treated with great love and gentleness, and the Angels and Spirit Guides I meet have the demeanor of loving grandparents. It is an absolutely wonderful, peaceful feeling, and I hope you experience it for yourselves someday.

Those three experiences are the most significant and emotional ones I can remember. I was taken to another level, so to speak, and I have faith that it was all real and shown to me for a reason. The fact that I don't understand it doesn't matter. My soul understands, accepts, and appreciates what takes place. I'm the eavesdropper, merely along for the ride. And what a ride it has been! I am no longer afraid to die because I know that we don't truly die. Our souls go on to live in Heaven where we are happy and healthy, engaged in countless educational and spiritual pursuits, and that we stay aware of the lives of our loved ones still here on Earth.

And that sounds like Heaven to me. In the next chapter I'll share some examples of just how aware Spirit is of what is taking place in our lives.

seventeen

My Readings

I used to talk to a psychic or psychic medium once a year as part of my spiritual development, or as I would say "for entertainment purposes." In reality, I sought confirmation of what I had been seeing, hearing, and experiencing. When my Angels, Guides, and Departed Loved Ones were identified by name, or specific events in my life were discussed, I knew that I was on the right track. I didn't offer information or react to what I heard, and the spiritual communication flowed.

This chapter offers you a glimpse at the type and quality of information I have received with well-known, very gifted psychic mediums and authors. I want to share my experiences. All of what follows is taken from my handwritten notes during sessions or while listening to audio files and tapes sent by the psychic mediums. I hope to give you an idea of what a visit from Angels, Spirit Guides, and Departed Loved Ones is like. I also want to remind you that you can receive this sort of information yourself—if you are open to the experience and practice, practice, practice. After reading this chapter you may realize that our Departed Loved Ones are still alive and well in Heaven, and they keep track of us and our lives here on Earth.

I read Rebecca Rosen's wonderful book, *Spirited,* and received a message while meditating that I should schedule an appointment with her. I visited her Denver office in March 2011 for a St. Patrick's Day small group reading. Her messages for me were interrupted by an anxious Spirit, so I signed up for a second small group and brought my wife along, as well. That reading was terrific, and when Rebecca indicated that there were still more messages from my Team for me, I scheduled a phone session.

After going years without a psychic reading, I had three in six months, and I'd like to share some examples of what I experienced during these sessions. I realized that Spirit continually jumped in and out during my reading, so I decided to identify the individual, our relationship, and compressed their messages.

As you read these, try to imagine what type of information your family and friends, Angels, and Guides have for you.

Rebecca was an absolutely delightful young woman—funny, warm, and personable. She would look up at the ceiling to receive messages from Spirit and then at the recipient to deliver them. Two women who came together received a twenty-minute message from their husband/brother. He knew what they discussed in the car and what song played on the radio as they drove there. He told his widow that she would meet an older man in five years and remarry, and that it was fine with him. I imagined that spared her some future doubt or guilt. This was the ladies' first attempt at anything like this, and I told them they just received a gold mine of information.

One woman's mother came through and spoke about alcohol quite a bit. Apparently she was still attending monthly get-togethers in a bar with her daughter and granddaughters, and she said that she liked the cocktail screen saver on her daughter's computer. Rebecca graciously asked if the mother in Spirit was an alcoholic, and—to no one's surprise—she was.

A young woman flew in from San Diego and burst into tears when Rebecca relayed a message from her boyfriend, a motorcycle racer who had passed in a crash. That was difficult to see and hear.

Two women sought information about finding love, and this seemed out of place. Most people came to learn about Departed Loved Ones(DLOs), and these women were looking for Mr. Right. In both cases, they received messages from Spirit Guides, and no DLOs came through.

A young man came through and repeatedly showed Rebecca the number twenty-one. She said that this young man looked about that age and asked a dark-haired young woman if she knew someone that age that had passed or if that number meant anything to her. The lady burst into tears and said she had lost her son when he was twenty-one months old. He came through with a stern, yet spiritually and politically correct, warning not to leave her young daughter alone again in the bathtub and to give her swimming lessons when she was older. This lady was being "called-out" by her son in Spirit, and I got a strong impression that she was responsible for his passing.

The attendees were very excited to hear from their Departed Loved Ones. They laughed and cried. Some were thrilled to hear the messages, while others couldn't bear it.

I believe that people's reactions depend upon their stage of grief, and how recently their loved ones passed. I tell people that they can go into Rebecca's small group reading and not believe in contact with the Other Side or that our DLOs live on in Heaven. However, after hearing Rebecca deliver detailed messages for over two hours, as well as seeing the attendees' reactions, there is no way they can leave and not believe that they have witnessed after-death communication.

Al, my father

Rebecca mentioned that she had a male who died of lung issues, and I immediately said it must be my dad's brother, who died of lung cancer. She said that this Spirit said, *"Wow, is this real?"* Then she said, *"No, it's your dad. Al says that you will not have the same issue."*

My dad, Al, died in November 1968. He was in the hospital for pneumonia, and his heart gave out. Here it was March 2011, and I had had two brief contacts with him in twenty years of meditating. Rebecca said that he was tearing up and getting emotional. He wanted me to know that he was no longer stoic, and he regretted that he didn't say what he wanted to say to me. Rebecca said she didn't recall experiencing such an emotional Spirit, accompanied by his Spirit Guide for support. Dad said that he has watched me with my sons and that I was doing an incredible job of being open, kind, giving, available, and generous. Al was taking notes from me and said that I redeem him. He'd done a Life Review and said that I was the older soul in our dynamic. I was stunned and silent. The rest of the group stared at me, and reacted with compassion to my dad's message.

Dad regretted his lengthy hospital stays. He had withheld things because he didn't want to burden me. He went on to say that his mother, *Mary*, and Terry's father, *Bob,* were there with him. Dad and Bob never met while incarnated, but they know one another in Heaven.

Dad talked about *Emily*, his wife and my mom. I always called her Ma, but I upgraded it to Mom for the book. And he talked about her losing a baby when she was eight months pregnant, one of three miscarriages. Rebecca smiled as she mentioned sparks of light appearing behind me. I didn't remember Mom losing a baby in her eighth month, but it may have been when I was about eight years old. I have written in another chapter about hearing my parents talk about her two miscarriages during an in-utero regression with Dr. Brian Weiss, so the number three appears to be accurate.

Dad told Rebecca that he was there when I got the oil changed in my car the day before. I laughed and said that I was alone in the waiting area of the Grease Monkey, and the annoying smell of cigarette smoke had me on my feet and searching for the source. Dad came through and told me he was trying to identify himself.

Dad told me not to change my job and that I should stay long enough to reach my potential because there was a pot of gold— a Big Thump— coming. He was not just saying it; it was in my contract, set up for five years from now, and it was a genius moment. That was the reason I stayed in screenwriting for so many years. Dad said that he was the messenger in this.

My contract referred to my Sacred Contract, a spiritual to-do list of all the things that we wished to accomplish during our latest incarnations. As I typed this, my Big Thump was still apparently two-and-a-half years away. Lucky me! Dad, could you see if you can move it up a little? I've always said that those on the Other Side have no concept of time.

From my later meditation notes:

"The pot of gold and Big Thump references are to a book based on your work with us in the future; how(your mission)was brought about and guided by God's Hand through His Angels and Spirit Guides."

Rebecca looked up at the ceiling, then back to me, and asked about the number twelve, and if I ever see 9:12 on a clock.

I started to laugh. "Twice a day for twenty years now."

I told her September twelfth is my birth date. She said that seeing it validated me and meant that I was on path and in alignment doing what I needed to be doing. When Chris and Joel were growing up, I'd constantly look over to the closest clock at precisely 9:12 and yell out "Yoo-hoo! 9:12! Happy Birthday to me!" It got to the point where my family members were so sick of hearing it that they'd tell me to just shut up.

Mom had a problem with remembering my birthday. After all, she did have two children, so how could I expect her to remember my sister's birthday—and mine—every year? That's why I shout "9:12!" whenever I see it as my head mysteriously swivels to the nearest clock as those magical numbers appear.

It was amazing to hear from Dad. He needed this time to express his regret, although to me it was unnecessary. We always had a great relationship, and I'd never felt anything but love for him. He was very sick for a long time, and he lived two years longer than expected. He was a gentle, quiet man, and I didn't hold it against him for not talking about his eventual death to a young teenager. I always wondered why he didn't visit during my meditations over the past twenty years. Perhaps he was busy enjoying Heaven, and—remember when he first came through—he was surprised to be able to make contact. I felt sad that for forty-three years he carried this burden that he had somehow let me down.

On my second visit, Rebecca said that a father, Al, was there and asked whose birthday was on 9/12? She looked around the room, and I waved at her. She laughed when she recognized me from four months earlier. Then she asked who had a coyote in the backyard, and she said that a father was bringing it through. I waited for everyone else to deny the coyote reference before I raised my hand. I was reading on our patio when a coyote appeared from a ravine and stared at me until I screamed, waved my arms, and chased it away. Rebecca said that Al was responsible for it. He and Bob(Terry's father)get a kick out of my fear. Real funny, Dad.

Dad spoke of my two sons, Chris and Joel, and said that he is connected to both of them. Chris has grown up to look a great deal like Al.

I found photos of Al and Chris, both at twenty-one, and every facial feature was identical. Al said that he was thrilled to talk to me again after his visit in March and that he was a strong soul mate to Chris. He was his Spirit Guide, they were meant to look alike. Of course, they never met. Al passed over in 1968, and Chris was born in 1980. Al went on to say that Joel was a very wise soul who "gets it" and was comfortable talking about spiritual stuff. He was "on path" and that Terry and I should listen to him. As I sat at my computer and typed this past section, I suddenly lifted my eyes and glanced across the room at the digital clock on a bookshelf. The time read 4:25—Joel's birthday. As I read my two-year-old notes where my Dad said that my son was "on path," I saw Joel's birthday on the clock. It's 9:12 all over again with this family!

Al told Rebecca that he was one of thirteen children and that his siblings were all standing there with him. He was so happy to be reconnected with them and was closer than ever to all of them. He said that I was reaching to a Spiritual Path, versus a Religious Path, and that it was OK for me to be different from him and Mom—that he gave me his permission.

Emily, my mother

Mom passed away in 1990, and she remained quietly in the background during these three sessions. I believe that was because she has come through over two hundred times in earlier meditations. Now she stepped up and showed Rebecca a bouquet of roses for me to express her love. She said that she was also involved with my sons and not to give Dad all of the credit.

Mary, my paternal grandmother

Mary came through twice in the three sessions, yet I had never heard from her in twenty years. She told Rebecca that she had a special interest in me and that I didn't recognize why I'm still here on Earth and not in Heaven. Rebecca said that I had had nine lives and believed that someone was looking out for me, like Mary and some Higher Spirit Guides. That's for sure.

Rebecca asked if I had had open-heart surgery. I hadn't, but I did have a serious heart attack and angioplasty in 2000. Mary told me that the heart attack was an Exit Point and she was glad I decided to stay. It wasn't my time, and I had good times and good work ahead of me.

Mary said that she loved to crochet, did it often(try ten hours a day), and that we had some of her work. There was a box of lace doilies in our garage. Yikes, was I caught by Grandma in front of fifteen witnesses in our group, and who knew how many in Heaven?

Bob, Terry's father

Rebecca opened the small group reading with tidbits that she received during her meditation an hour earlier. She mentioned that Bob was there to see his daughter Terry. Bob thanked me for bringing his daughter to the second small group session. He said he often saw Terry when she worked in our yard, and planting and being in Nature were like meditation for her. He said that he would send a deer to Terry as a way of saying "hello" to her. Terry was puzzled and recalled no "deer connection." Days later, as she drove out of our neighborhood, a deer stepped out from the farm across the road and stopped in front of her car. It looked right at her as they both did a "you go, no, you go" dance before it walked away. Not only did Terry see a deer, she interacted with it. Thanks, Bob.

Bob said that Terry was doing important work. Rebecca said that she saw a nurse's cap and asked if Terry worked in health care. Bob said that Terry impacted others with her presence and energy, and Ruby (Terry's mother) added that she hadn't recognized it but saw it now. My wife had thirty-five years of experience in health care management and executive positions, and Bob's remarks were spot-on. Whew, I almost said dead-on.

Bob talked about boating, fishing, and a lake. He told Terry that *"His Heaven"* looked like their small lake behind their home in Miami Springs, Florida, and that she could *"go there"* if she closed her eyes and revisited her memories. He put down a golf club and said that he was not into golfing—that he had lots of good friends there and gets along with Ruby. They see eye-to-eye now.

Ruby, Terry's mother

Rebecca said Ruby is delightful and beautiful, and even though Terry was not close to her Mom, she's highlighting herself and offers Terry roses to say how much she loves her. Rebecca added that Ruby was always the center of attention – all about me – and she has not changed. She says that she has lots of family there that she never thought she'd see again. (Ruby passed away fifteen years before this reading and has visited with my Mom to say hello during my meditations dozens of times even though they never met while here on Earth.)

Rebecca chose her words carefully and said that Ruby is not a deep Spirit and hasn't fully risen to that level. I take that to mean that she is fully enjoying her time in Heaven but not taking advantage of the opportunities for spiritual education and advancement. Terry is the older soul, the teacher and parental figure to Ruby, who now understands it. She says that her ego was too much in the way to give Terry that credit, and then she showed Rebecca scenes of Dorothy from *The Wizard of Oz*. As a young woman, Ruby resembled Judy Garland, so this was confirmation that it was her.

Bob and Ruby come back to mention that they would send coins to Terry as a means of saying hello to her, and we often found them around the house. Better coins than a deer, Bob.

Angels and Guides

Rebecca told me that she saw *"a whole Team in Spirit of Guides and Angels here with you. Wow!"* Great, that's why I came— to receive some outside confirmation of things I'm told during my meditations. She was really awed by the number. This had happened to me before with psychics. I'd been told, *"You bring a lot to the party."* As she began to relay a message from my Team, she suddenly looked confused and asked me who David was. *"You know, seventeen-year-old David."*

Now I'm confused too. Rebecca turned to a woman across the room and said that David was here for her. She looked back to me. *"Sorry, I have to go here now."*

And my time was over, done, kaput—mere seconds before I was about to receive the information/confirmation/validation that I had driven hundreds of miles and spent hundreds of dollars for. It seemed David committed suicide, and across the room his grieving mother had been waiting her turn, but David couldn't wait and jumped in. When I heard the details and saw her reaction, I understood. She needed to receive this message from her son, and he needed to tell her that he was sorry for what he had done, for her pain, and to let her know that he was alright now.

Similarly, my dad had needed to come through and deliver his message with the support of his Spirit Guide. How could I feel cheated? How could I begrudge her the opportunity to hear from her son and feel the joy and happiness I had just felt when my dad had come through? This mother had become a Grief Counselor following her son's passing.

I later found the following messages in my journal: *"We were there and stepped aside to allow a more urgent message to come through for the grieving mother from her son... your father was there working on his guilt issues. Everything she said was correct. Mary(my grandmother)was there for support, as well as his Guide and Bob. Believe what your father said. Be glad you were there for him. It helped him tremendously, and you had no idea it was part of your Sacred Contract."*

My Guardian Angel, David added, *"Your visit with Al made you realize your guilt is unhealthy and holding you back from moving forward."*

In my 6/28/2011 meditation notes, my father, Al, popped in and said, *"Thank you for going in March so I could speak with you. I'm doing great now. I needed to let you know how much it bothered me."*

David and Arianna, my Guardian Angels

My two Guardian Angels, David and Arianna, appeared before Rebecca. They were a continuing source of love and comfort to me. Whenever I was in their presence I felt great joy and was thrilled to be welcomed by their all-encompassing hugs and smiles. They were gorgeous beings and must have been almost ten feet tall. They said that it was time for me to awaken my Sixth Sense and Spirituality. Although I am able to go deeply into meditation and sleep, I am jolted out of it and awaken. They wanted my permission to take me Astral Traveling when I was sleeping. I should surrender fear and control and let them take over. Great, go for it!

My Angels instructed me to set my intention and thank the Universe. During my meditations when I discuss this matter I am repeatedly told, *"In God's Hands, in God's Time, Dear Paul."*

Sounds like a catchy title for a book, doesn't it?

Rebecca mentioned that she could spend a whole hour with me later, but she had to move on. Terry and I stayed after the group reading and chatted with Rebecca. I shared some of my experiences and mentioned the book title I had been told to use in the future. Her face lit up, and she said it was such a great title. Rebecca suggested that I get on her cancellation list for a phone reading and that it was twelve-hundred-strong.

A few days later I decided to do it, and I asked my Angels to bombard Rebecca with messages to tell her to speak with me. I registered via e-mail for a thirty-minute phone session on a Friday morning. The following Monday I received an e-mail about an opening available in thirty days. I accepted it immediately. Do you think I jumped over twelve hundred people on the waiting list in three days? Or do you think that David and Arianna came through for me?

Yeah, so do I.

Dan, my Spirit Guide

Rebecca said that a male Spirit came through laughing, and said to call him Tonto—that I'd never guess who he was. Of course, I know that it's Dan, my fun-loving Spirit Guide who had made himself known to me and every psychic and psychic medium who had ever read for me. Rebecca asked about ringing in my ears, and "Tonto" confessed that he's "the ear thing" that I believed was tinnitus. Spirit was trying to change my vibration field to vibrate higher and faster and to connect better with them. On the drive home from Denver my left ear fizzled, then popped, four times, and a month of ear ringing ended. No doctors were needed, just one Spirit Guide.

In my September 8, 2011, telephone session, Dan came through with a few Spirit Guides. The Guides laughed and said that I gave them a run for their money. They described being involved in areas of my life, such as my writing projects and psychic abilities. They also referenced my near-death experiences where I was kept on path and choosing life. One kept reminding me of my purpose and held me to my Sacred Contract. In my experience, Guides would come and go, working with me in certain aspects of my life or during specific time periods. Sometimes I would meet with Guides during my meditations and "listen" to what they had to say without learning their names or remembering what they said. I take it on faith that my consciousness absorbed their instruction for use when necessary. I learned that my Spirit Guide, Dan, has worked with me lifetime after lifetime. He showed Rebecca my *Book of Life*, and says that he knows everything about my Sacred Contract. He is, of course, the same one who teases me about looking into my Contract only to show me pages that are blank or written in an ancient, undecipherable language.

Spirit encouraged me to go to a spiritual retreat in Arizona or New Mexico to be with like-minded people and absorb the high energy. Rebecca asked if that made any sense to me. It did. I was considering a "Celebrate Your Life" conference in Arizona that Terry and I attend about every two years. This message sealed it for me and I registered immediately. We had a wonderful time and parts of what I experienced at the conference are mentioned in other chapters.

I was told not to put too much pressure on myself to get everything done. I should be productive, yet have fun – keep my balance, and be light. They say that I have a very playful, laidback energy, which I agree with so I'm glad they noticed.

In summary, my thirty minute telephone session expanded to forty-five, and I received information that applied to what was happening in the lives of my wife and sons, and for me both personally and professionally. My two Guardian Angels and Spirit Guide came through, and brought along four additional Guides. My parents and Terry's came through, as well as three of my grandparents and five relatives and friends. Most of these people died over fifty years ago, and I was too young to know who their friends or deceased relatives were. When I was a child we had four generations of family, around seventy-five strong, living in the area, so keeping track of the living ones was difficult enough.

In total, eighteen Angels and Spirits made their presence known during this session. Their detailed information could not be researched or found on social media. It clearly was sent by Spirit and received by a very gifted psychic medium. Do you see how busy this session is, with all of the Departed Loved Ones, Angels, and Guides stepping forward to pass along a treasure of very detailed information? They just couldn't wait to be heard.

In the Houston area, Kim O'Neill, another wonderfully gifted, psychic medium and author, provided me mostly very personal and career-specific information in several phone readings, along with a recording of each session.

I'll share some favorite highlights:

A) *"Angels help with your writing. It's your life's work. Your career will explode in 1997."* I sold a movie-of-the-week to ABC, and it did very well in the ratings. My career didn't explode, but it burped.

B) *"Spirit begs you to hire a CPA. IRS has tax questions."* Yes, they did. I made a mistake with a dividend on our return.

C) Spirit showed Kim the Gold Cross vision I had when, after many requests for a sign, I was given an unmistakable one, yet I still didn't believe it.

D) Spirit quoted me for Kim, *"Living in (my town) is like being buried alive in The Twilight Zone. The town is discouraging, draining, and depleting me spiritually and creatively."* My Guides chuckled that I was like *"the turd in the punch bowl"* and the *"odd duck,"* and that I *"have no spiritual contracts here."* Amen, enough said.

E) Spirit gave Kim accurate information about one of my heart procedures. My Guides said that there would have been no time for
a bypass—only in an emergency—and that my heart was *"good
enough."* I had the procedure done three days later and woke
from the anesthesia to hear my two doctors discussing another
patient who was arriving in five minutes, and there was no time
for a bypass. Kim sent me a tape where Spirit foretold the doctors' conversation.

F) My Team of Angels and Guides had changed over the years.
I started with 102, then 111, then 112, and now 114 members
who worked with me. So much of my sessions with Kim dealt
with messages regarding interest in my writing and the people
involved, as well as specific Guides who assisted me with these
projects. These Guides spoke to me in the middle of the night
with suggestions for scenes and dialogue.

What would you give to hear from your Departed Loved Ones,
Guardian Angels, or Spirit Guides—to receive information that they
were alive and well on the Other Side, and paying attention to your
life? My father and Terry's mother came through and expressed regrets
for their perceived failings, even though we didn't feel they had let us
down. I was thrilled to know that my parents were helping my sons,
and both sets of parents were enjoying being reunited with family and
friends. They said they even played cards together.

Have you been to a reading from a psychic medium? Do you think
the information you receive there is accurate? Does the contact *feel*
real? You can't fool your soul! If you can afford one, I recommend that
you try it.

I shared my first reading with Rebecca Rosen to a woman who had
recently lost her mother. As I spoke, I had a vision of a late scene from
the film, *Field of Dreams*. It appeared with a message for her—a message
from Spirit:

"For its money you have and peace that you lack."

Peace that you lack—did that just hit a nerve? In my dad's case, he was the one who needed to make peace with his guilt and with me. Without a reading we might never had made such a remarkable contact, and his healing might never have taken place.

Do you believe that maybe our Departed Loved Ones are still aware and involved in our lives? Through psychic mediums, Spirit spoke of an amazing variety of topics from family, health, career, hobbies, and relationships, to details of conversations and my tax mistake. This information feels authentic and connected to my life, and reinforces my belief that my family and friends in Heaven are still engaged in my life. Perhaps death does not mean good-bye, but rather, 'til we meet again.

What do you believe? And what are you willing to try?

I read that it takes twenty-seven muscles in your face to frown, but only two to smile. That's over thirteen times more effort to be negative than positive, and I'm positive that my spiritual life is much richer and more evolved because of the presence of Angels, Guides, and Departed Loved Ones.

Perhaps this chapter is your wake-up call, if you were curious about readings and considering one. Speaking of wake-up calls...

eighteen
Wake-up Call

*"There are no other opportunities available to you.
You have promised this life to God and must wait
until He decides the time is right to proceed."*

A wake-up call is a kick in the pants from Spirit. It puts an exclamation point at the end of an event to make sure that you don't miss the lesson. It guides your focus to its intended direction.

My wake-up calls involved two visions of the brown car hanging in the air, my near-drowning and miraculous saving, the sudden death of my mother by cancer whereby I needed to know where she went after she passed (*"She can't just be gone"*), and my choking near-death experience followed four months later by a serious heart attack.

Why did I need so many? I must be pretty slow compared to others, so these wake-up calls were meant to push me continually forward and prepare me spiritually for my destiny, mission, or special purpose—whatever you want to call it.

All of these wake-up calls inspired me to begin reading, attending seminars and workshops, visiting a hypnotherapist and then psychics and psychic mediums, and finally making contact on my own with my Angels, Guides, and Departed Loved Ones. Each one of these "rungs" on my ladder furthered my spiritual journey.

The point is, if I can do this, so can you. If I were any different, I may have needed fewer reminders. Once again, you have to make the effort. Perhaps reading this is your wake-up call.

I have a literal wake-up call story. I was in Tucson and meeting a friend for breakfast at ten. I awoke at six and took a drive around the area before returning to my hotel room at nine-thirty. I stretched out on the bed and asked my Angels to wake me up in fifteen minutes in case I dozed off. I did, and fifteen minutes later my eyes sprung open in time to see a pillow hurtling down towards my face. Thanks, but a gentle nudge or whisper would have sufficed.

My last wake-up call may have been the final nudge I needed to write down the experiences of my spiritual journey. It came when I decided to investigate the Miracle in the River and was the latest big event I've experienced.

nineteen

The Miracle in the River, Revisited

*"This is all a test, a school to see
if you can withstand the lessons you must learn
in order to fulfill your destiny."*

Twenty-two years later—in June 2012—Joel and I returned to Steamboat Springs and the Yampa River to investigate the miracle that saved my life, sent him back from the White Light, and to see if we could find some answers.

A very gifted Energy Healer near Aspen told me in March 2012 that I needed to get over my fear of water. This was odd since we weren't discussing anything related to it. He just picked up on it after four visits over two years to work on foot and hip issues. I shared my "hole-in-the-river" experience, and he listened intently. *"God has plans for you,"* he said softly. Surprisingly, I've heard those exact words from a few listeners to my story. *"God has plans for you."* It seems like they are delivering the same message to me. At a workshop, I handed my copy of Neale Donald Walsch's magazine to him, opened to the first page of my story, and he wrote, "Paul, God has you" across his introduction.

I told the healer that I panic in hot tubs or if water gets up my nose in the shower, and he suggested that I needed to combat this fear. I decided to go back to Steamboat Springs for the first time in twenty-two years. I would find the hole and throw in a weight tied to a marked rope to measure the depth.

When I told Joel of my plan, he wanted to go, too. He didn't think I should go alone, and his abruptly-changed work schedule would allow it. He said that he was thinking about it a lot lately and had recently found copies of the satellite images I had sent him three years earlier—plus he'd bought a new camera that he was eager to try. After twenty-two years, we were going to make our first return trip to Steamboat Springs to investigate and confront our miracle—and my fear.

The day before we went, I meditated, and when I "arrived," I was surprised to find my Angels and Spirit Guide standing on the tip of the small island in the river. I was shocked. We were in the exact spot where I materialized before the two kayakers—the ones who screamed and left me. I wonder if they'd ever told their story about how a large, wet man had materialized out of thin air ten feet away from them. He was kneeling, choking, and gushing river water, and they just paddled away, screaming. Somehow I doubt those two were, or have ever been, First Responders.

From my meditation notes, here are some of the messages from my Angels and Spirit Guide:

"We'll be here tomorrow. You want to get over your fears. Take photos. If you get Angels in your photos, or, Guides, perhaps this will start your work with Joel, and this may open doors for you… Enjoy your day and adventures with Joel… you are happiest with your family, are you not?"

I turned the journal over to see the next message I had scribbled via automatic writing.

"You will not have any traumatic experience tomorrow—just measurements and photos, then lunch, and go to the waterfall for more photos. You'll both be pleased."

Reading that fifteen months later, I don't understand why the words *"traumatic experience"* didn't raise any red flags for me or why I didn't question it immediately, because a traumatic experience is exactly what I had twenty-four hours later.

Joel and I arrived in Steamboat Springs in time for an outdoor lunch at a creekside restaurant. Afterwards, we went to investigate. We were looking for an overpass with a concrete wall, close to a small section of rapids and not too far from the small island. The water was rushing hard and was much deeper than the eighteen inches we dealt with years ago. The slopes leading down to the water were covered with large, jagged boulders, and getting down there to locate the hole in the riverbed and measure its depth would be very difficult.

I looked down at the rocks and thought that there was absolutely no way I was going to be able to do it. We decided to begin our investigation by going down to the tip of the island, where there was a small riverfront park. We parked on the main road and walked along a paved trail onto a bridge over the river to the island. We tried to get down to the island, but we couldn't reach the tip because of the dense undergrowth, so we decided to go just to the opposite bank. From there we would be maybe twenty to twenty-five feet from the tip of the island. Perhaps we could even walk across to the island, depending upon the depth of the water. Once there, Joel would take photos, and we would see what turned up since he'd had great success capturing phenomena in his photos.

We walked down the sloping riverbank that ended with a ledge just two feet above the dirt. The water was then only fifteen feet away. Joel went down first and jumped, landing upright on both feet. I stepped down to the edge of the ledge and hesitated. Immediately I felt very ill at ease. Should I jump? Should I sit down and scoot on my butt down the ledge, or kneel down and go down backwards like a toddler on a staircase?

While I stood there deciding the safest way to maneuver, I suddenly felt, and then saw myself jump down. It was surreal. I hit soft, sandy dirt, and then I heard a very loud crack. I collapsed forward, dropped to both knees, and hit Joel's back with both hands in a desperate attempt to break my fall. I rolled over onto my side and then my back, and looked up to see Joel's face as he looked down at—then turned away from—my left ankle. I snuck a quick peek, and it was horrific. My left foot was turned to the left at a ninety-degree angle.

A man on a bench above us saw and heard my fall, and called the rescue squad. They came in a few minutes to take me to the hospital, where X-rays showed that I broke my ankle in three places, my leg in two, tore tendons, and, oh yes, my left foot was no longer connected internally to my leg. Surgery was delayed for a week because one of my heart medications needed to be cleared from my system.

Joel later said he was about to turn around and tell me not to jump because of the sandy dirt, but it was too late.

The thing was—I had no intention of jumping, yet I did. I never consciously decided to jump, but somehow my body left the ledge, I dropped and fell, and destroyed my left ankle. What made me jump before I made that decision? I could have easily sat down and scooted down the ledge. That's how I got back up the slope by lifting my elbows to shoulder height and raising myself up so I could be put on the stretcher and gurney. Very confused and in shock, I started babbling to the rescue workers about my experience there twenty-two years earlier.

They thought I had lost my mind, and this was the reason people who have had experiences like mine tend to keep them to themselves. People don't believe you, so why open yourself up to their disbelief and ridicule? When we left the hospital, I asked Joel to return to the island to take some photos since our investigation was over and I didn't want to leave empty-handed. That was one of the reasons for the trip to Steamboat Springs. In my meditations I had been instructed to return to the spot where my life was miraculously saved in June 1990—to combat my fear of the incident and to take photos. The indication from my Angels and Guides was that they would appear in the photos.

As I waited in the backseat of my car with my leg elevated, Joel went down to the riverfront park and took photos. When he returned, one shot especially caught our eyes. A fluffy white cloud showed a floating Angel with its hands held before it in prayer. You can see the pointing fingers, upright thumb, forearm, upper arm, shoulder, and a head and face in profile as well as two tiny wings on its back. The rest of the body diffused into cloud. The Angel's dark hair was encircled by a wreath. The image looked familiar to me. I found my copy of Doreen Virtue's *The Angel Therapy Handbook,* and the artwork on its cover depicts an Angel with short dark hair and a wreath around its head—just like the Cloud. I asked Joel to give me a copy of the photo as a Father's Day present, and it currently sits on a bookcase in our home office. Whenever I look up from my desk and computer, I see it and marvel. How cool would it be to have a photo of the "Waving Angel" Cloud framed next to it?

Here's an interesting fact about the photo: Joel took another wide-angle photo of clouds just twelve seconds earlier, according to his new camera, and our Angel Cloud was not in the sky. So where did it come from in twelve seconds?

I meditated five days later and was pretty upset that my Angels and Guides didn't warn me about my accident. In fact, if you remember, they said, *"You will not have any traumatic experience tomorrow."* I broke my leg and ankle, and tore everything but my Achilles tendon, but they didn't consider that *"traumatic?"* I guess that's what happens when you need to investigate God's Miracle instead of accepting it on faith.

From my automatic writing notes of June 6, 2012:

"You would have gone to a point in the river that was very dangerous, and an Exit Point would have come up for you. We didn't say anything because of your Free Will, and your life wasn't in imminent danger at that point like before. But you would not back away once you proceeded, and you would have continued on, and a tragedy would have occurred. Your Soul decided to jump, not your Conscious Mind. You did it to save yourself from more serious injury."

At this point they showed me a vision of my body sprawled across jagged rocks with a fatal head wound. Blood poured out onto the rocks, and from my expression I knew I was dead. It was not easy to see myself like that, and in a few seconds the image disappeared.

"We are very glad that you survived. Do not be afraid. Surgery will go well. Your recovery will go well. Take this time to prepare your book on your experiences and to work on your (mission)."

Here's some information that I didn't need to hear:

"Don't go back to Steamboat Springs so you won't be tempted to try again."

No kidding, and no problem. Then they said:

"Look for us in the hospital and before surgery. We'll be there to offer support."

I didn't see them in surgery or my room like I had in 2000. In the operating theater I passed out from the anesthesia the moment I shifted from the gurney to the table.

I believe my soul pushed me off the ledge in order to prevent me from proceeding further into a dangerous situation that could have ended my life. It was a preemptive strike, perhaps similar to the one the Brown Car had when it slid off the icy road before it drove into the blizzard.

Let me explain the concept of Exit Points. According to my many wonderful books on spirituality, when we plan our next incarnation on Earth while on the Other Side, we select times when we can announce that our stint here is finished, and we are ready to return Home. We've had enough of this life and find ourselves in situations such as illnesses or potential fatal accidents where we can easily "give up the fight" or believe that we have accomplished enough of our Sacred Contract or Chart.

My scenario in the hole in the river was an Exit Point, but I clearly was not ready to leave my family. My serious heart attack was another Exit Point, as well as the choking incident four months earlier. In addition, I have been warned eleven times of potentially serious or fatal auto accidents. These may have been Exit Points, as well.

In 1975 in England, I was following a large semi on a two-lane winding country road at night. The driver of the lorry, as they called them, waved me on, indicating that it was OK for me to pass him. I pulled out alongside of him to see another lorry bearing down on me and not stopping or slowing down. I had only a few seconds to make a decision, so I pulled my little Triumph Spitfire as close to the first lorry's side as I could and probably went a little beneath it. The second lorry sped past and for a couple of seconds I was caught between the two speeding trucks—just holding on tight to the steering wheel and hoping to survive. I didn't hear any warning from a disembodied voice then. Maybe I had "a feeling" to slide over and under the lorry a bit, because it probably saved my life that night.

Our Contracts, or Sacred Contracts, are written along with our Spirit Guide, and we choose the things we want to work on in our next lifetime on Earth—our challenges and life lessons, our strengths and weaknesses, our family, friends, and coworkers, our interests, skills, and abilities, our geographic locations, our appearance, our health and illnesses, etc.

Take a moment to examine your own life. What challenges have you faced that you wished you hadn't? What people are in your life that you wish you'd never met? Do you have any health issues or career problems? What have you learned from your experiences?

Can you imagine the coordination required by our Spirit Guides on the Other Side to get everyone to agree to come into our lives for a season, or a reason, or a lifetime? Think of all the people you've encountered over the years and the impact they have had, both positive and negative, on your life. Now imagine everyone's Spirit Guides up in Heaven negotiating and coordinating, dates, places, and length of time so we may teach or learn from the other person.

At the very least, I know from what I have experienced, seen, and heard on my personal spiritual journey that I am on path with my Sacred Contract. I am here in order to love and raise my two sons, and care for, love, and protect my wife as I failed to do in previous lifetimes. I am here to explore my own spirituality and experience the loss of my business career.

I love how Sylvia Brown explains that writing our chart while in the love and safety of the Other Side makes us overconfident and that it is like shopping in the grocery store on an empty stomach. Who hasn't made that mistake? Who hasn't regretted their choices and actions and wished for another chance, another direction, and another opportunity to change the course of their life? Why did I have to choose such a difficult life? What on Earth was I thinking?

Sorry, it should be *"What in Heaven was I thinking?"* If you had made those choices on Earth you would have been less brave and more realistic in what you hoped to accomplish.

Four weeks after my "accident" I meditated and asked what I was supposed to do over the summer months. From my meditation notes:

"Write your experiences down, and then you will decide whether it is to be a novel or an autobiography of your spiritual years."

I then asked why my injury was so severe.

"To keep you(home)and immobile to do the spiritual work necessary at this time. This is the way God chose. Start writing. Have fun. It will all flow easily out of you. Memories will flood in. We'll give you a nudge."

I then asked about my experience in the hospital and seeing Spirits in our home.

"You are beginning to see Spirit Guides more easily as a part of your advancement. Do not doubt the experience. You can communicate with them as you sleep and remember some of what they say... they are with you to guard you during this period of your life."

Regarding my waiting room experience after surgery where I saw huge test tube trays holding clear, oddly-shaped tubes containing "squished" men and women:

"Yes, the waiting room was real. Souls could escape the trauma of the body and reenergize here with us in Heaven. Your healing is going well. There will not be any problems or follow-up surgery, so ease your mind."

Two weeks later during another meditation, my Angels and Spirit Guide made their presence known early on. I sat on my recliner and asked that they appear and give me guidance. With that my MP3 player flew off my lap, hit the floor a few feet in front of me, and turned itself on to my meditation tape—and not to any of the twenty or so music CDs.

I retrieved it, put in my earphones, and began to meditate. I immediately felt pressure in my Third Eye. When I "arrived" in a flash of white light, I found myself in my old school, where I met twenty years ago with thirteen Spirit Guides in a large, cathedral-like building with many similar groups of humans and Spirits. I was greeted by my Guardian Angels, David and Arianna, and my Spirit Guide, Dan. Standing behind them was my "Team" of Spirit Guides who over the years had worked with me and revealed themselves to psychic mediums. We exchanged hugs and hellos and then my questions and their responses began. Here is a small portion of what they said:

"You are on path. Write your experiences. Do not delay. Learn that you must wait for the Divine Timing to be perfect."

I spent months rereading my books on spirituality from my favorite authors and jotting down notes of my experiences. I didn't feel ready to sit at the computer and begin writing until fourteen months later.

Terry brought home Dr. Mary C. Neal's book, *To Heaven and Back*. One evening I opened it to a random page that held a very specific message for me:

"I knew what I was supposed to do; I just didn't want to do it."

Dr. Neal went on to say that she was supposed to share her experiences and life stories and use them and her observations to help others stop doubting and just believe. And that seemed to be a mini wake-up call for me to finish this project.

As I typed that last sentence, I glanced at my 2012 journal and saw that Spirit had turned the page of my meditation notes— as if to affirm Dr. Neal's message by taking me to their own earlier one.

"Please begin writing your experiences and stop delaying the inevitable. Let it flow, whatever shape it takes. Get your experiences down for your family. It will be just fine. Just do it! You have been on this spiritual journey. It will awaken your soul. The lamp "clicks" are our energy near to you. Don't doubt or compare yourself to others. You are touched by the Hand of God. Do not worry about timing. God knows what you need and want. Let Go, Let God. Go now to the Healing Temple, and let Raphael work on your legs. Go in God's Peace and Love."

How cool was that? On my desk was a pile of notebooks, books, and folders, and as I was typing, my "Team" managed to change the page to enable me to see an appropriate message.

And that, Dear Readers, is how my life is—a stream of little "hellos" from my friends to help in some way or just to make their presence known. I receive little, personal tidbits of information, guidance, and answers to my questions, also known as Spirit Communication, or signs, that I'll share in Part Two.

PART TWO:

Spirit Communication

Signs, Signs, Everywhere Signs

Spirit communication comes in many forms, and I've compiled the various ways that my Angels, Guides, and Departed Loved Ones have been in touch with me through the years. What follows are some personal examples of the efforts Spirit makes to get our attention—even if we're not trying to make contact or asking for a sign. Sometimes you'll be very relaxed with a clear mind, and they feel the time is right to sneak in a little "hello," and then you experience a "Did-that-just-happen?" moment.

Perhaps you have and brushed them aside. Relax and ask Spirit for help in remembering any signs you saw but didn't actually notice.

I dare you.

"Look for more visits from Angels and Guides, and for messages from them. Have faith! We are working with you and on your behalf."

twenty

Angel Clouds

On a beautiful, sunny and cloudless September Saturday afternoon, Terry and I sat and read on the patio as we enjoyed our flowers and visiting birds. Terry jokingly said that perhaps an Angel would appear before us since I always asked that if they appeared they should stand on the far end of the field behind our yard so I wouldn't be scared. I have had issues with Spirits appearing out of nowhere or walking through our home without saying a word. I dozed off for half an hour, and when I awoke Terry laughed and said that she hadn't seen any Angels. I nodded and then looked up at the sky. "There it is."

I pointed to the southwest directly in front of us. Off in the distance, maybe five miles away, a lone, wispy, white gigantic cloud hung between where we were and the canyon walls of The Colorado National Monument. It was an Angel Cloud, perfect in shape and form, and easily one mile long. From left to right we saw a long, flowing robe, complete with many folds, two smallish wings on its back, and two outstretched arms with open hands and ten distinct fingers clearly in view. The head was a hollow circle with curly ringlets of hair cascading around it. We stared, awestruck at this obvious response to Terry's request. "Maybe it will wave to us," Terry joked, as she gave me a "Can-you-believe-this?" look.

"Don't be a smart aleck," I sort-of-said. "Watch." In seconds, the outstretched, lower left arm and hand receded back into the chest, collapsing until it formed an oval in the heart area of the chest. The head slowly turned to look down at us, and wisps of cloud quickly formed eyes, nose, and a mouth. The face of the Angel appeared to look directly at us, as if saying *"How's that?"* Suddenly, sunbeams burst through from behind the cloud, shot out from the "oval heart," and then spread out and illuminated the deep blue sky.

Terry told me to get the camera, but I refused to leave. I wasn't about to take my eyes off this wondrous sight. She ran into our office and returned moments later with the camera.

The Angel Cloud was still there, looking down on us in all its glory.

"Oh damn, the battery's dead," Terry moaned when the shutter wouldn't open. In an instant, a wind blew in from the north, and the Angel Cloud quickly began to collapse into itself from right to left. First came the extended right hand and arm, then the head followed by the torso—which cut off the radiant sunbeams—until the flowing folds of its robes turned into a small, fluffy ball of a cloud. Finally, it dissipated, and we were left once again with a clear, blue, cloudless sky.

Since the camera wouldn't work, I believed that we weren't meant to capture this amazing display. Terry asked for an Angel to appear, and one did—only not in the shape or location she had asked for. I ran inside and made my best attempt at recreating the event— "my best" being poor for even a disinterested kindergartener. I drew both versions of the Angel, first with its outstretched arms, and again with one extended arm and the filled-in face and heart. I still have the drawing buried in the closet. Terry and I will always have the wonderful memory of her asking to see an Angel and that magnificent Angel Cloud appearing before us.

From my meditation notes:

"You'll have more visions and thoughts to prepare you. Your heart's desire shows you the future. We put the Angel in the sky to show you that we are in your life, and you are on path."

Here's another Angel Cloud story that ties into the photo Joel took above the spot of my "accident" in Steamboat Springs.

Three weeks later, I rested on the living room sofa with my left leg in its cast raised on a pile of pillows. I looked out the dining room window and sliding glass door into our yard and the nice view of our field, the farms beyond that, and the canyon walls fifteen miles away.

It was another gorgeous June afternoon, and the blue sky was dotted with billowy white clouds. I glanced out the tall dining room window, and, at the edge of a large cloud, I spotted the face of an Angel in profile, along with its neck, shoulders, and wings.

"Is it real, or am I imagining it?" I asked aloud to no one except our sleeping cat, Millie.

Suddenly, in response to my questions, three huge bursts of light struck the Angel's face from the south. They looked like bulbs exploding from an old-fashioned flash camera. Timed about three seconds apart, they highlighted the face.

"Yeah, it's real. I saw it." I laughed and watched as the face collapsed into itself and was absorbed by the rest of the huge, billowy cloud.

There is a medical term for the brain's ability and efforts to see—or make—faces where there usually is none. I accept that; however, I get the feeling that Angels and Guides can do whatever they want, and I'm just lucky enough to see what they allow me to see. If I doubt that I once again saw an Angel Cloud, how do I explain the three flashes of light that illuminated the face three seconds apart? How does that possibly occur in Nature? It doesn't. I accept this as another sign from my Angels that they are, indeed, in my life.

twenty-one
Angels and Death

Most of us have Loved Ones who have passed away, leaving those who remain behind to grieve and wonder if they were alone or if someone or something was with them. I have a few stories I'd like to share.

One of my aunts passed away in her sleep, as did a friend's grandmother. Each was found in bed looking at the ceiling with one arm outstretched and their fingers open, as if reaching for something. I believe that Spirit came to guide them Home.

I first met my brother-in-law, Brian, in his hospital room in San Francisco, where he was living and suffering from ALS, or Lou Gehrig's disease. His doctor said that he would be OK for about two years, and then she called the next day to tell us that Brian could no longer walk. We flew out on a Friday morning and visited with Brian for three hours in his hospital room, went for a walk so he could nap, and returned to find him in a coma. Brian went from "being OK for two years" to a coma in just two days.

On Sunday evening, Brian had been lying on his right side with his eyes open for fifty hours. I told Terry that his soul was probably running all over San Francisco having a great time while his body was here in bed. As we were leaving his room, I paused at the door, turned back, and asked for Angels to take care of Brian, as I said good-bye.

Brian's right arm slowly lifted off the bed from the elbow, and his limp hand gently waved to me. It was obvious that he was not controlling the movement. It was too limp, and he couldn't even close his eyelids, much less lift his arm.

I smiled through tear-filled eyes, and we left, happy in the knowledge that Brian was not alone. The next morning we received a phone call at five a.m., informing us that Brian had passed in his sleep.

Weeks before Brian's passing, I meditated and was taken by my Angels to Terry's and Brian's mother in her hospital room. Ruby was being treated for pneumonia in a Florida hospital. She was sprawled across the bed in her gown and robe and looked terrible and near death.

Instantly a young man with dark hair appeared before me, and Ruby disappeared. He smiled and excitedly rubbed his hands together. I was upset because his delight seemed inappropriate.

I turned to my Angels and said, "I have no idea who this is." In an instant a wedding photo of Ruby and Bob, her husband, flashed before me. I had seen it in Ruby's living room when we last visited.

Bob continued to smile and move around, very happy, and one of my Angels told me that he's excited because Ruby is coming Home soon. Suddenly I was whisked away, and on to another session with my Angels. I didn't mention this to Terry that evening because, frankly, I didn't know how.

"Hey, I met your dad today, and he's really thrilled that your mom is joining him soon." See? It doesn't work.

The next afternoon Ruby's doctor called to say that she had passed from a heart attack. I had to break the news to Terry, and the only comfort I could offer was that I knew Bob was waiting to guide her Home.

Arrival Party

I have meditated and been escorted by my Angels to see newly-departed family and friends being greeted in Heaven by crowds of happy, excited well-wishers. I call this celebration an "Arrival Party," and I'd like to share some experiences with you.

On the day my grandmother died I meditated, and my Angels took me to her arrival on the Other Side. My grandmother stood with my grandfather, who had died thirty years earlier, and they faced a large semicircle of family and friends, all laughing, talking, and welcoming her Home.

The crowd noticed me standing with David, one of my Guardian Angels, and some motioned for Grandma and Grandpa to turn around. They did and were amazed to see me with an Angel.

"Paulie! What are you doing here?" Grandma shouted. Grandpa leaned over and whispered in her ear. She nodded and turned back to me.

"Hey, this ain't so bad. Look, I got my Vally back." My grandfather's name was Valentine. Then turning back to the folks in her Arrival Party, she said, *"I gotta go,"* and waved good-bye to me. I was then whisked away to another location on the Other Side. I had made contact with my grandmother just a few hours after her passing and was able to witness her joy and excitement at being reunited in Heaven with her Departed Loved Ones.

Grandma's *"This (Heaven) ain't so bad"* remark was typical of her. Waving me off with an *"I gotta go"* was, too. I left Buffalo to join the Air Force, attend college, and start a career. Whenever I returned home and saw her over the next dozen years, Grandma would always give me a quick *"Paulie, hello. How you doing?"* and then go back to another conversation as if she just saw me a few days earlier.

Now that she's made it back Home, nothing's changed, except that she's reunited with her husband again and thrilled to see so many old friends.

I made contact with my stepfather, Andy, weeks after his passing. I purposely waited for a while to meditate so I wouldn't interrupt his Arrival Party in Heaven. Andy passed seventeen years after Mom did, and I never mentioned to him that Mom was in contact with me. She said not to tell the family because they wouldn't be able to handle it, so I didn't. Why would I do anything to jeopardize this after-death communication I'm fortunate enough to experience?

Back to Andy and our initial contact. He came through with Mom, and the first thing he said was, *"Why didn't you tell me about this sooner? I never would have waited so long."*

I recalled my last visit with Andy was when he was in a Buffalo-area convalescence center. He had had four heart attacks in a month and was in bad shape. I spent a week with him, and we chatted easily in his lucid moments. At other times he'd introduce me to the nurses as his brother-in-law. Every evening as he drifted off to sleep, I'd ask if Mom, or his departed parents, had come to visit him—as my dad and others had come to visit Mom. He said that they hadn't but didn't seem to catch on that they had all passed years before. Andy crossed over in his sleep four days after I returned home, but I'm sure he wasn't alone when it happened. No one is.

I was meditating three weeks after one of my aunts crossed over and crashed her Arrival Party. She turned around, gave me a playful scowl, and shook her fist at me, as if saying, *"You knew about this and never told me."*

Mom said not to—so there, I'm good.

One more Arrival Party story involves a family friend named Ken. He and his wife moved out of state, and we lost touch with them. One afternoon I meditated, and my Angels took me to the Arrival Party of a dark-haired man in his late twenties. He stood before a large semicircle of Spirits, all eager to speak with him. They paused and motioned for him to turn around and look at us.

He did and seemed confused. So was I. I didn't recognize him, so I turned to my Angel and said, "I have no idea who this is." Immediately a photo flashed before my eyes—one of a young man in his college sweater with a large letter "A" on it. I recalled that Ken had graduated from the University of Arizona and mistook this for his son. I didn't meet Ken until he was nearly fifty so I didn't recognize this younger version of him. His friends in Spirit explained what was going on, and he offered a very little smile and a brief wave and then turned back to his group.

This was very different for me. Usually, when I'm taken to one of these Arrival Parties, I stand about ten feet behind the guest of honor with my Angels, but this time I was probably one hundred feet away and floating in the air—a first for me! I remember feeling wobbly and scared, and we left immediately.

That happened on a Friday afternoon, and we learned of his passing in the Sunday morning newspaper. After his funeral, I pulled his wife, Sherry, aside and shared the story of my visit to his Arrival Party.

He has since popped in twice during my mediations by stepping into view from the far left and looking sheepish, as I say my good-byes to my Angels and Guides. He asked me to tell his family that he was fine and loved them. Terry came home from work one evening and said I'd never guess who called her out of the blue.

Wanna bet? "Sherry called you," I said confidently.

Terry was astounded. His wife called and asked for help with a retirement issue. Terry followed up with her the next day and was able to pass along her husband's message of love.

The Guests of Honor of the Arrival Parties I've seen all appear extremely happy, healthy, and very pleasant. Some appear as they looked when they passed or the same age, and others much younger. Maybe they have a choice in their appearance. I've needed my memory refreshed many times, since Spirits whom I'd known on Earth in old age have appeared before me as young adults. Someday we'll all be the Guest of Honor, and I'll be young and thin, maybe even cute. How about you? Hey, it's your party. Go for it.

What I've been shown by my Angels confirms that we don't die alone, and we are immediately greeted by Angels and Spirits. We are whisked away to Heaven, where eager Departed Loved Ones await to celebrate our arrival. I hope that information will someday lessen your grief after a loss.

twenty-two
Where Did It Go?

Whenever I can't find a personal item, I ask my Angels and Guides for help in locating it, sometimes with remarkable results. Usually I receive sudden knowingness or a vision of the item, and then I know exactly where to look.

One afternoon, Terry misplaced her car keys. She dumped out her purse onto our bed three times and searched through the contents with no luck. I suggested that she ask her newly-departed mother, Ruby, for help. She did, dumped her purse again, and all the contents tumbled out, including her car keys. Thanks, Ruby.

I couldn't find my house keys once, and my family knows, I never leave without my keys, nor should anyone. After a failed search, I told Spirit that I had given up. I then had a vision that my keys were on the passenger seat in my car. I ran out to the garage, and there they were.

Last winter I came into the house and hung my coat in the hall closet. I placed my German hunting hat—a smaller version of an Indiana Jones fedora—in its usual space on the shelf where I keep my scarves and gloves. Later that day when I went to retrieve it, it was gone. I began a frantic search but admitted defeat, and then I asked Spirit for help. My head swiveled, and my eyes were drawn to the left one of two closet doors. Terry kept her coat collection there so I never opened the left door. I walked over, opened it, and there it was, up on the left side of the shelf, just sitting there—mocking me. Another little "hello" from my Spirits.

Living in Colorado's dry climate, I am a slave to my lip balm and usually keep it in a tray above the refrigerator. One day I couldn't find my tube of Chapstick anywhere—and I mean anywhere. Not in the pockets of my coats in the hall closet or my pants in the master bedroom closet, or lying in the tray on the fridge. I searched until I was supremely frustrated, gave up and decided to leave. As I walked away, I heard, *"Look again,"* in my head. My head and eyes swiveled back towards the fridge, and I saw that the tube of Chapstick was standing upright on the hinge of the refrigerator door. There was no way I would have missed it during my search!

My Spirits have fun with teabags. In May 1999, I was brewing a cup of tea on the kitchen counter. Terry had just accepted a new position, and we would be moving across the state. I closed my eyes as I held the tag of the teabag and gently swayed it from side to side so it slowly moved within the hot water in the cup. I asked my Angels for help with the move. "I want to find a nice house. I want to get a good job. I want to buy a new car." I was interrupted by a voice that said, *"And now you want a teabag."*

My eyes sprung open, and I looked down at my cup. I was still swaying the tag—the string was still moving back and forth—but there was no teabag at the end of it! And it was nowhere to be found. Not on the kitchen counters, not in the sink, not on the floor, not in the breakfast nook or any other room on the first floor. Unbelievable. And just how far could it have gone as it slowly swayed, confined in a four-inch-wide cup? Was it Dan, my playful Spirit Guide, having more fun at my expense?

The next morning I was upstairs in the master bathroom brushing my teeth and thinking about my vanishing teabag when a vision flashed in my mind's eye.

It was the missing teabag. MY TEABAG. I'd recognize it anywhere since it no longer had a string and tag attached. It sat perfectly centered on the third step leading down into the basement of our open stairwell.

I threw down my toothbrush, raced down the stairs, and there it was-MY TEABAG! My no-tag, no-string teabag rested exactly where I had seen it in my vision. It sat there, taunting me after twenty-four hours of hell. Our boys had their own family room in the basement where they played video games, watched television, and entertained friends. Note that I omitted "did their homework and studied." This was a high-traffic area, and there was absolutely no way this teabag could have laid there and gone unnoticed.

My litany of "I want, I want, I want" was heard by Spirit, who then happily gave me one more thing to want. Lesson learned, or maybe not. A few unhappy years later, I found myself standing at the kitchen counter and once again brewing a cup of tea. I absentmindedly held the tag of the teabag and gently swayed it from side to side within the cup. As I recited a new list of "I wants," I remembered my last teabag experience and then opened my eyes and glanced down at my cup. The teabag was still there, only this time it was fully above the cup and out of the water. As I gently swayed the tag and its string, the teabag hung there, absolutely motionless, as if an unseen hand held it steady. I just started to laugh, looked around and said, "OK, now I get it." Lesson learned—finally.

I always ask my Angels and Guides to give me a sign if they're around me. Sometimes they do nothing at all, and other times their response is dramatic. Too dramatic.

One morning I was minutes away from a doctor's appointment and a trip to the bank. I stood in the middle of our family room with its high, peaked ceiling and looked around at the four rooms I could see from that vantage point. I asked my Angels and Guides to give me a sign if they were with me, and then I waited. I looked around—nothing. Fine, I thought, it's time to go. I walked into the kitchen to retrieve the checkbook and pen I had placed on a long, empty counter minutes before. When I reached the counter, I picked up the checkbook, but the pen was nowhere to be found. Gone, baby, gone.

I retraced my steps throughout the house. Where could I have put the pen? Then it dawned on me. *They* took it. I stood once again in the center of the family room and looked around, while I laughed. "I asked for a sign, and you stole my pen? Big deal. I'm not impressed."

Just then, I felt a whoosh of air as something dropped down past my right ear. I flinched, then looked down to see my lost pen as it bounced off the carpet a few times before coming to a rest near my feet. "OK, now I'm impressed." I retrieved my pen and headed for the garage.

But Spirit wasn't done. *"You want a sign, Paul, we'll give you a sign,"* they seemed to say in hindsight. Two minutes later I sat first in line at an intersection and waited at a red light in the right lane. A monstrous white pickup truck was on my left and blocked my view of northbound traffic. Above its hood I could see the trees and their high branches next to our bank, catty-corner to my westbound position.

The traffic light turned green. I took my foot off the brake pedal, barely rolled forward, and heard *"Stop!"* shouted from just behind my left ear even though I was alone. I slammed on the brakes and avoided a collision with an old pickup that had run the red light and sped past my car.

I caught my breath, and then I moved my foot from the brake to the gas pedal.

"Look out!" the same voice shouted again from behind me. My head swiveled up and to the left. My field of vision now focused on the tree branches near my bank. As I looked above the high hood of the truck to my left, I saw a large windshield with a man up near the branches. Shocked, I slammed the brake pedal a second time as a cement mixer sped through the intersection past me. Had I not been warned by Spirit, I would never have moved safely through the intersection.

I sarcastically said, "Big deal, I'm not impressed," when they returned my pen. Little did I know that two minutes later I'd be in a position where they may have saved my life.

Let me tell you, I was impressed, very impressed.

And very grateful.

One more lost item story, and this is a Big One, a two-parter that involves my beloved Movado watch disappearing in front of me.

For years in the 1990s I would gaze at full-page ads for the classy and stylish Movado watches. I knew that one day I would own one. Often, I would casually flip open a magazine to the exact page and see the ad.

I finally bought a Movado and wore it for years, and when it started looking a tad worn, I bought another. I just love the simple, handless design with the black face and gold sun at the top. I was confused, angry, and then devastated when it disappeared in front of me in February 2010. I bought that second Movado watch when my stepfather, Andy, passed away and considered it a gift from him so it held special meaning to me.

I visited my son, Joel, in Denver, and on a Sunday morning we met for breakfast at the Original House of Pancakes. Afterwards we stood by my car and chatted, mostly about my recent spiritual experiences. I half-jokingly complained about the promise I made to God before my miraculous rescue with the remark that if you make a promise to God, remember to put a time limit on it. I didn't have much time, or any leverage, to negotiate while drowning and neglected to do so.

I was approaching the twentieth anniversary of my near-drowning, and I was still waiting for God to use me as I have been shown over the years in meditations. I told Joel that God, the Angels, and my Spirit Guides don't "do" time in Heaven, then I checked my Movado and saw that it was 9:20 a.m. I had a four-hour drive through the mountains ahead of me, if I-70 was clear of snow and ice.

Once home, I sat on the living room sofa and read the Sunday paper. Terry was running errands, and I was watching a basketball game on the television. My watch began to bother me, suddenly pinching my wrist. I slipped it off, placed it on a pile of newspapers on the ottoman in front of me, and returned to my reading.

I finished the sports section, and reached to the ottoman for another section of the paper only to see that my Movado was gone! Gone where? Gone how? I had taken it off and placed it three feet in front of me just minutes earlier. But it was nowhere to be found. I searched the entire car, too, with the thought that the clasp broke while I drove home.

I searched my clothing and suitcase, and I tore apart the living room by moving anything that I could. I repeated the process for three days since I get pretty anal about missing items. I even called the motel I stayed at and asked them to search my room and check their Lost and Found. It wasn't there either.

What I didn't do is think that my Angels or Guides would steal my watch. Please, they knew how much it meant to me, and I was positive that I removed it while reading the paper. Simply put, I removed my watch, placed it down three feet in front of me, and the next time I looked, it had disappeared.

I called upon my Angels to bring it back to me, just as they had done before with the tape of the psychic telephone reading from Houston. Unfortunately, nothing happened, nor was anything revealed to me when I meditated.

My Movado was gone but not forgotten.

Twelve weeks later, Terry and I were in Florida visiting her cousin. Terry had gone to bed, and Eleanor showed me an ABC special about miracles she had recorded. She said that my experiences were as good as the folks interviewed, and we settled in to watch. I had shared many of my spiritual experiences and after-death communications, including those involving her parents, and she thought that I'd be interested in the program. Of course, I would. I certainly have an open mind about these things.

Something on the television jogged my memory, and I started to tell Eleanor about my visit with Joel and complaining about my promise to God, the considerable time that I've been waiting to fulfill it, and my disappearing watch.

As I spoke, Spirit leaned in very close behind my left ear, and a man's voice said loudly, *"We took your watch to show you that time doesn't matter."*

Whoa, baby! With that I jumped up, ran across the living room, and stopped next to the television set.

"Did you hear that?" I shouted, totally freaked out.

"No. Hear what?"

"Someone just said, 'We took your watch to show you that time doesn't matter.'"

"No, I didn't hear anything," Eleanor replied, obviously confused, but she had the presence of mind to "pause" the recording. I was hyper, breathless, and frightened as Spirit answered my complaints in a clear and direct manner. I looked down at the television and the image onscreen, and then pointed and shouted, "Look at that!"

Onscreen, the picture was frozen. Against a clear, blue sky, was a billowy cloud in the perfect shape of an Angel, standing in the center of the screen and facing forward with its hands outstretched. "Look at this," I cried. "Do you see the Angel?"

She did. It was so clearly an Angel Cloud. I made her run the recorder back and forth, again and again, to see if the special on miracles included this Angel Cloud as a part of it. It hadn't. The program had transition shots of fast-moving clouds to designate time and location changes in their stories.

"We took your watch to show you that time doesn't matter." That statement was proven by the appearance of an Angel onscreen at the exact moment Eleanor paused the recording. It appeared for only the two of us to see, mere seconds after I received an answer to my twelve-week mystery. It was an acknowledgment that my Angels took my watch to teach me a lesson and that they were indeed with us at that moment.

Since then, whenever I ask when my work for God will begin, my Angels give me the same response, *"In God's Hands, in God's Time."* Sometimes they add, *"Dear Paul,"* at the end, and that's a clear message that my brain is not making this up because there is no way in Heaven or on Earth that I refer to myself as *"Dear Paul."* I lean towards more colorful adjectives and descriptions when speaking of myself. Use your imagination here.

I did replace the "lost" Movado watch and hope that one day my Angels will return the one they took. Another lesson learned, but still no watch.

Here's an update on this story. Three years later my daughter-in-law's cousin, Michelle, spent the night with us on her way to a Grand Canyon rafting trip. We sat in our home office and discussed my spiritual experiences, once she saw the Angel Cloud photo taken where I broke my ankle and leg.

I was shocked when Michelle offered one of her own experiences. She had a vision of an oncoming car that just vanished as it drove towards her one winter night. She stopped her car and searched along a dark mountain road until she found an overturned car in a ravine that was not visible from the road. It was a white car in a snow bank. She asked me if Angels could have told her to stop and search.

Of course, they did. First they showed her a vision of a disappearing oncoming car to get her attention (as they had with me in 1989), got her to stop her car, and search in an isolated area. Her quick thinking and actions probably saved a woman from freezing to death that night, since five rescue vehicles were summoned and the jaws-of-life were needed to rip open the car's roof. We met Michelle the week before at our son's wedding and offered her a place to stay to break up her long drive. I truly believe that she accepted our hospitality in order to provide the right setting for her to share her experience and to confirm her suspicion that Angels employed her that night to save a woman's life.

Back to my story: As I told her of my Movado's disappearance from the ottoman, she blurted out, "They took your watch to show you that time doesn't matter."

She quoted my Angel, just substituting "they" for "we." Was it a coincidence? How could she possibly know what I was about to say? How could she possibly quote a message from my Angels? It's called *knowingness,* where a thought is placed in your head and you receive information you wouldn't otherwise know.

The next morning at breakfast, Michelle told me that, when she returned to the Denver airport after the wedding and waited for a shuttle bus, a man fell forty feet from the level above her and landed ten feet away. Her quick response alerted emergency services as she prevented this seriously injured man from being struck by oncoming vehicles.

A second coincidence, you ask? No way. Angels recognized her as a person who would not hesitate to provide assistance and again positioned her to help yet one more person in danger of losing his life.

Michelle's stories are not about lost items, but about Spirit putting the right person in the right place at the right time to help someone who has lost his way.

What is missing in your life? Love? Hope? Faith?

What have you found in your life? Friendship? Spirituality? Faith?

Have you ever asked for help, and did Spirit answer the call? They have for me—acting like mailmen in the next chapter titled Special Delivery.

twenty-three
Special Delivery

Angels and Spirits are able to use mail as a way to make sure we receive information or support when it is needed and requested. And since I'm always asking for guidance, help, or signs, I have two stories I'd like to share.

In 2001, my thirtieth high school reunion was coming up in Buffalo, New York. I was ambivalent about going and concerned about the expense for a weekend trip. I was on the Internet to check flight times and car rentals, and Terry told me just to go. I said I would, only if money suddenly appeared out of the blue, and we both agreed. The Saturday mail arrived moments later and contained two unexpected items—a dividend check from our insurance company and a residual check from the WGA—more than enough money to cover the trip.

The other instance came after a telephone session with Houston psychic medium, Kim O'Neill. She recorded our session and sent a cassette tape of it. I appreciated this service since the information flowed so quickly that my notes covered only half of what she relayed from Spirit. After ten days the tape still hadn't arrived so I called and spoke with Kim. She told me that her husband delivered the tape to the post office in a padded mailer the day of our session. As she spoke, a vision flashed in my head. It showed the padded mailer trapped between a wall and a large, heavy metal cart on wheels. I was very frustrated and asked my Angels to bring me the tape. I didn't care how, just do it because there was so much information from my Angels and Guides that I needed to hear again.

I suddenly had an urge to go check our mailbox. Inside was the padded envelope from Kim—my missing tape! Here's the cool part. The envelope was pristine, with not a wrinkle from its journey from Houston to western Colorado, and the stamps had not been cancelled by the post office. There was no little red circle with the date, city, and zip code. It seems this envelope bypassed the U.S. postal system completely after I asked—OK, whined to my Angels—for help.

And the "normal" mail delivery came an hour later.

I'm going to lump in a UPS story with the Mail category, even though UPS was the sworn enemy of my mother and stepfather, both of whom retired as U.S. postal workers. My mother complained that UPS even "stole their initials," meaning UPS is derived from USPS. Some nerve.

On 9/12/2008, the Denver Broncos played the Buffalo Bills, my favorite team, on my birthday. I hadn't eaten any Polish food for years, so I thought it would be fun to invite sixteen neighbors over to watch the game and share the "food of my people." I found a company in Buffalo that sold and shipped Buffalo food favorites. These perishable items were shipped UPS air, and I expected two boxes to arrive on the Friday before the Sunday game.

The boxes didn't arrive on Friday, and on Saturday morning I began to panic. I got on the UPS website, tracked my shipment, and tried to confirm that it would be delivered that day. I discovered that it had been left behind in the hub in Louisville, Kentucky for a day and now sat in the Denver Airport.

I called the UPS customer service folks and learned their Denver facilities were closed for the weekend, and that my boxes would be delivered on Monday afternoon, twenty-four hours after the game. Lucky me. Sixteen guests were coming, and my birthday gift—thank you very much—sat spoiling at the Denver airport, two hundred and eighty miles away.

After a rather stressful conversation, I started to check recipes online so I could recreate the Polish entrées I planned to serve. As I listed the items to buy and stores where I could find them, I again asked my Angels for help.

"Angels, just put my food on the Grand Junction delivery truck and get it here now." Simply put, I wanted two large boxes of perishable food items to bypass the regular delivery route from Denver International Airport to the UPS hub in Commerce City, and then to be transported across the Rocky Mountains to Grand Junction and finally to our home. Easy.

A few minutes later, list in hand and still pretty upset, I headed out to run my errands. I opened the door into the garage and froze.

Two large boxes with UPS air stickers sat on the step and blocked my path.

Holy Cow, it worked! There they were, my two missing boxes that, according to the tracking info on the UPS website, were still at DIA. I was truly excited and explained it all to Terry, as we unloaded the divine Polish food I would feast on for the next ten days. I sort of made too much, so it was a good thing I liked leftovers.

There's more. I ran into neighbors who saw the UPS truck stop and the driver carry the boxes into the garage. I ran an earlier errand and left the door up, so there was confirmation that the boxes were physically delivered by UPS and did not "just appear," like the padded mailer from Houston.

On Monday, I got back onto the UPS website and tracked my shipment again. Guess what? Apparently it was still at the Denver airport. There was no record of it ever moving to the Denver hub, to Grand Junction, or to the delivery truck, and then to my home. Nothing. Nada. Zilch.

I asked my Angels to put my food on the delivery truck and, Good Heavens, it appears they did just that or else they manifested a UPS truck and driver, as well.

Either way, I got my Polish delicacies and had a great time. Happy Birthday to me and a big *Thank You* to my Angels!

The next time you need a "special delivery," I hope you remember to ask Spirit for assistance. What have you got to lose?

twenty-four
It Was Here A Minute Ago

⸻

Apportations involve the movement of objects manipulated by Spirit. I call them little "hellos" from my Angels and Guides, and I have some stories for you. Some cross categories and are mentioned elsewhere: stories about the psychic reading tape that arrived from Houston, the teabag on the stairs, flying books, and the Chapstick on the corner of the refrigerator.

Walking into our master bedroom closet to change my shirt, I removed my eyeglasses since I had to pull my polo shirt over my head. I placed my glasses on a built-in shelf on my right, about chest high. I put on another shirt, and when I turned back to retrieve my glasses, they were gone. In thirty seconds, with me standing in the same spot, they disappeared.

I searched the room and was upset that I must have misplaced them somehow, but after all these years, I knew Spirit was playing a prank on me. Finally, I closed the closet door, moved a hanging bathrobe, and pushed aside six pairs of my pants that were hanging on an eight-foot-high bar so I could move a stack of winter sweaters I piled on a shelf three months earlier.

And there, leaning between the sweaters and the wall, were my eyeglasses—about ten feet across the room from the shelf where I placed them. How did I even know to look there?

So if Spirit didn't move my eyeglasses, I must have come into the closet, closed the door, moved the bathrobe, slid pairs of pants on hangers aside, moved a pile of sweaters, and stood my eyeglasses against a wall. Doesn't everyone?

And then I forgot about it thirty seconds later, right?

In 2000, we bought a wood-and-iron park bench to place next to our front door. I assembled the bench on the floor of the garage and sat with the bench parts scattered to my left and the instruction sheet to my right. As usual, I asked my Angels and Guides for a sign that they were around me, hoping that one day they would just give in and reveal themselves to me in the flesh so we could have a normal conversation.

Confused by the parts, I turned back to the instructions and found that the sheet of paper was gone. I searched the garage and didn't find it anywhere. There was no breeze so it didn't fly away, and it was only a foot away, so where could it have gone? It was very strange.

Three weeks later I was getting ready to mow the lawn, and again asked my Angels for a sign that they were with me. I grabbed the grass-catcher to attach to the mower, and when I lifted it, the instruction sheet floated out. It teased me and stayed airborne for an impressive amount of time; as if an invisible entity waved it around to taunt me. One more thing—it was just as clean as it could possibly be.

After I cut the grass three times and emptied the clippings numerous times, how could that instruction sheet have been in the bag and not have a single green stain on it? I asked for a sign and got it—stolen instructions and one slightly lopsided bench.

On Sunday mornings I like to make a pot of coffee to drink while I read the paper and have breakfast. After I shook grounds from the Starbucks bag into the filter, I stood at the counter and carefully folded the open top of the bag downward. I hadn't noticed that the bag had a tear in its side, so as I folded, my beloved Columbia Medium Roast poured onto the floor and formed a neat pile near my left foot.

Seeing this, I became upset that I had wasted so much coffee and that my wife would enter any second, notice, and then I'd have to answer her inevitable questions about the mess on her floor. I immediately said out loud, "Angels, just don't let Terry see it," as I stepped over to the refrigerator, and put the Starbucks bag inside. Then I grabbed the coffee pot, walked over to the sink, reached for the faucet, and froze.

Sitting in the sink next to the drain was a small mound of dry, ground Columbia Medium Roast. I spun around and looked down at the floor across the kitchen, where the coffee had been, and it was completely clean. Then I looked back down into the sink, saw the coffee, and then back at the coffee-less floor, again and again, as I tried to make sense of it. I finally realized what happened and looked around and up to thank my Angels for their help, just as Terry, unaware, entered the kitchen.

If Spirit had put the spilt coffee back into the Starbucks bag, that would have been a miracle. I can't win them all.

Terry attempted to meditate in the late 1990s with poor results. She either received no information or fell asleep. On two occasions she was in bed reading and told me of her frustration, as I stood across the room at the door. Her complaints appeared to have been heard by Spirit because the first time she complained, a small stereo that sat on a headboard shelf fell off and hit her on the head. I watched as it tumbled down. Luckily, Terry was OK.

The second time she vented, a small television set on a corner table toppled over, a few feet from me. It caught my eye just as it shook, and then flipped over.

I guess the Spirits had an issue with her frustration and let her know that they were there listening. The lesson here is that if you say that you can't meditate, you are right because you won't be open enough to receive any communication from Spirit. Have a mind that is open to everything and attached to nothing is what Terry always tells me. Ironic, isn't it?

Years ago we were at my wife's work conference in a resort near Boulder, Colorado. My son, Joel, came to visit for the day. I mentioned something about a meditation and my Angels to him, and how I always ask them to give me a sign if they are near me. As I spoke, the double closet doors opened and closed violently, and the inside light went on and off for thirty seconds. Amazed, we stood and stared. Terry emerged from the bathroom and asked what all the racket was about.

"Angels. I asked if they were around, and it appears they are," I said innocently.

"Well, tell them to keep it down."

You should have seen those doors go wild. These things are over quickly, and while most are not frightening at all, they do leave me wondering if it actually just happened.

To me it's just another little "hello" from my Angels or Guides. Are you ready to ask Spirit for a sign that they are present with you? Sometimes that's all it takes.

twenty-five
Say Cheese

Spirits tap into our energy and make their presence known in a variety of ways. In my case and my family's, it takes the shape of orbs or balls of light, wispy energy or streaks of light, and ghosts or Spirits that appear in our photos.

My wife's employment identification badge has a head-and-shoulders shot of her standing in front of a blue backdrop. Well, that's the background in the photos of the other two thousand employees. Terry's is five percent blue and ninety-five percent wispy-white spiritual energy.

We have a photo of Terry taken on Joel's twenty-first birthday. In it, a large white orb hovers to her left, as she sits on his living room sofa. The orb is bright white and easily the size of a beach ball. A chair in the foreground has a large, butterfly pillow on it. My mom, now in spirit, collected butterfly art. Perhaps Mom stopped by for a visit. Once I began writing my notes on this topic, I discovered this missing photo after searching for years. There was no light source or reflective surface that could have caused the orb. None of us saw it at the time. It was only visible in the photo that my sister took, and she was certainly confused by it.

We visited Terry's mother, Ruby, in Miami in the mid-1990s, and my sons and I came across an old black-and-white photo shot in the backyard about twenty-five years earlier. Terry stood with her mother and grandmother on the grass in their backyard, in front of the large window of the family room. Standing inside the room about five feet above the women was Terry's grandfather. When I asked why he stayed inside, Terry said that he had died years before the photo was taken. Ruby had always said that she felt his presence in the house.

Sticking with Terry, we had Kirlian photos taken of us in Scottsdale, Arizona. This method captures the energy, or aura, of a living thing. Terry's photo showed an enormous white energy field emanating so close to her head that you couldn't even see her hair. It looked like a headdress Cher would wear in her Las Vegas show and was very impressive.

In our home office we have a photo of the gorgeous red rocks of Sedona, Arizona. Terry and I spent a couple of days there years ago. As we visited the shops and art galleries in this picturesque town, known for being a spiritual center, I clearly heard a voice in my head say, *"Find the Angel photo."*

Oh, great. Now I have to do it, I thought, since my Angels or Guides instructed me to do so. I wondered if it was going to fly off a wall and hit me in the head to get my attention. We visited every place that could possibly sell photos, and eventually wound up at The Church of the Rock. We went down into the church's tiny gift shop, and in a stack of photos, I found one and realized my search had ended.

In the foreground, or lower-third of the photo, was a desert valley, and three separate, gigantic red rock formations were in the middle-third. The top-third of the photo consisted of a clear, blue sky. Against the blue sky, and definitely in front of the rocks, are four wispy, yet distinct, pinkish-orange energy figures in the shape of Angels with huge wings.

I found the Angel Photo, as instructed by Spirit, and it has hung in our home office ever since. About five years ago, new neighbors moved in across the street—they came here from Sedona. I gave one a tour of our home, and she recognized my Angel Photo immediately. She was the gift shop manager at The Church of the Rock and had purchased the photo herself from the photographer. Coincidence?

About ten years ago I finally had an orb of my own in a Christmas Day photo. It was just a small white orb against my black sport coat. My one and only personal orb photo.

In 2009, I was back home in Buffalo, New York, to celebrate my birthday with my sister, cousins and friends. We took photos, around the dining room table. When I returned to Colorado, I loaded them into my computer and noticed a small white orb hovering in the living room in the background. I enlarged the photo and zoomed in on the orb. In an extreme close-up I could see the lower half of a woman's face, from her chin up to the bottom of her eyeglasses.

I couldn't identify the woman. Four families were represented at the table, and I'm sure the face in the orb belonged to my Mom or one of my aunts. They all resembled each other at a certain age, and all had children present at the party.

Joel is a terrific photographer, who frequently seems to capture ghosts or something unusual in his photos.

When he was five and his brother, Chris, was six, we moved to Denver and lived next to the University of Denver campus. On many evenings I'd take the boys to the nearby Observatory Park playground— the place to be on a summer evening. Across the street stood the Observatory, a two-story brick building from around 1900, with a large grassy field used for sports. About five years ago Joel took his newest Sony camera to Observatory Park to take photos of the playground of his youth, when he suddenly felt compelled to spin around and snap a quick photo of the Observatory across the street.

When you look at this photo on the computer and zoom in on the upper right window on the second floor, things get very interesting. Behind the windowpane there appears to be a man and a woman looking out. The man sits in a chair in overalls and a Henley shirt. The woman stands alongside him, with her left hand on his shoulder. She wears a dress and an apron that seems to be from the late 1800s. The man wears round, rimless glasses and has a very distinct physical trait - the top of his ears droop downward.

Another curious thing about the couple is that they are transparent. There is a wooden table behind them with a cardboard storage box on it, clearly visible as you look *through them*.

I zoomed in and saw four more figures, one in each quadrant of the window. I saw this photo recently on Joel's laptop, and in a much smaller version I easily picked out the pretty blonde girl with the curly hair and the naked baby boy who floated above her. There were four children in all, as well as the man and woman.

Joel did his research and found a 1929 photo of the astronomy professor who built the Observatory. He sits in a chair and wears round, rimless eyeglasses, and has the distinctive drooping ears of the ghost in the photo.

Three years ago, on a family vacation to Orlando, we took a day trip to St. Augustine. We toured the old fort, which was later featured on an episode of The Travel Channel's *Ghost Adventures*. Joel took his camera, clicked away, and got a couple of very interesting photos.

One photo of a cannon on an upper walkway captured the shadow of a man's arm coming in from the left. This presented a problem since there was no man in the area, and by the sun's position, the shadow was in the wrong location. So where's that arm coming from?

Another photo was taken inside a prison cell, where you had to enter by crawling through a small tunnel. Prisoners had been chained to the walls there. I felt very uneasy and refused to go inside with the others. When we returned to our condo that night, Joel reviewed his photos as I cut slices of key lime pie in the kitchen. "Dad, look at this," Joel said, as he approached the counter. I looked up, and from six feet away, I immediately spotted what he was referring to on the camera's viewfinder.

In the left foreground of the photo of the prison cell was a close-up of the profile of a thin-faced man with gray wavy hair, gaunt eyes, and a vacant stare. He wore a ruffled shirt and sat erect with his back against the wall. He looked like he was from the 1700s. It was as clear as could be, and just as creepy—an absolutely amazing photo. The ghost of a prisoner appeared in the shot, yet when it was later transferred onto the computer, the man's image disappeared. Still, we all saw it on the camera's viewfinder. Creepy, yet cool.

Joel took a photo of a headstone in a Denver cemetery. It seemed unremarkable in the e-mail he sent me until I hit the reply button. The e-mail window appeared in the center of the screen, and the photo changed size to reveal a tiny man standing at the side of the headstone or grave marker. He stood very low to the ground so I wouldn't have seen him otherwise.

This man seemed to be solid and stared at the camera lens. He wore black pants, a white shirt, thin black tie, and a black fedora. The man had a huge, long nose that gave him a creepy otherworldly appearance. He looked more like a fairy-type character than a human and couldn't have been more than a foot tall. It was unnerving to see this photo.

Central City is a former abandoned mining town and now is a gambling mecca in the mountains near Denver. Once again, Joel's camera caught ghostly figures that seemed to look at him.

He took a photo of an empty, two-story brick building from across the street, and he saw nothing unusual until he looked at the photo on his computer. He zoomed in on the four second-floor windows and saw ghosts in two of them. The more dramatic one revealed a dancehall girl, circa 1880–1900, I'd estimate by her clothing. She had one foot up on a wooden chair, and her ruffled skirt was hiked up as she smoothed out her stockings. Oh, one more thing: she was looking directly at the camera, not down, but on her eye level. This was strange because she was on the second floor while Joel was on the sidewalk across the street. The profile of a stern-looking, mustached man in a tall cowboy hat looked out from another window. There was also a photo taken through an open door in another building of what appears to be two "demon eyes" staring out from the back of the room. This is another very creepy photo. There must be something about Joel that attracts ghosts who want their pictures taken.

In May 2011, Terry and I took a vacation to Washington, D.C. We had never been there and were very excited to see the sights. Late one afternoon, we wanted to ride the elevator up to the top of the Washington Monument, but the last tour of the day was sold out. We walked outside, and I took a photo of the Monument looking up towards the west. It had rained that morning and gray clouds—light, medium, and dark—filled the sky.

Looking at the photo on our computer, I noticed in the clouds three distinct images that I never saw when I took the photo.

The Monument was in the center of the photo, and to its left, near the upper quarter of it, was a circular, bright white cloud. Closest to the obelisk, the left half of a man's face was clearly seen—his chin, mouth, nostril, deep-set eyes, and eyebrow ridge. He seemed to be facing the Capitol Building.

Emerging from the top of this bright, white cloud appeared to be the image of a shirtless man. You could see his upper chest just below the neck and some of his right shoulder. The face was at a forty-five degree angle, and his chin, mouth, nose, eyes, forehead, and hair were easily seen. His hair was pulled back into a little ponytail. Behind him, two faint yellowish wings extended from the cloud, and he appeared to be facing the White House.

The third image was in the lower half of the photo, below the round, white cloud and to the left of the Monument. Facing down towards the Monument at sharp angle, it was obviously a pig, or a Pig Cloud.

I've seen Angel Clouds, so why can't there be a Pig Cloud? This photo sits on my bookcase on a shelf below the one of the Angel Cloud, and I enjoy it immensely.

Are you eager to look through your old photos now to see what you may have previously missed? I can't be the only one who has Angels, Spirits, Departed Loved Ones, and other phenomena in photos, can I?

twenty-six
The Little Stuff

Spirit Communication comes in many forms, shapes, and sizes, and so do my experiences. In this chapter I share the smaller ones on my journey. As you read, try to remember if you have had any similar experiences, and please notice the variety of mine. Finally, ask yourself if this is something that you would enjoy pursuing on your own.

Akashic Records

The Akashic Records, also known as the Collective Unconsciousness, are the collective memories and records of every event, action, thought, word, and deed throughout history.

Over the years I have tried to get my Angels and Spirit Guide to allow me to go to the Hall of Records and sneak a peek at my personal information so I can get a preview of what life holds for me next. Clever, right? When I am escorted there during meditations, I find myself in a gigantic room stretching as far as I can see in all directions. There are many levels of metallic walkways, with an open lattice-like design so I can see through them far, far below—something which always frightens me.

Every time I arrive at a specific location, where a slanted shelf before me holds a huge leather-bound book, my book, which I believe holds the key to my future, in addition to information about my past lives. The only problem is, when I eagerly reach for my book(I don't see scrolls, just books)and open it, every page is written in a language I don't recognize. From my readings of books on spirituality I have come to accept that it is Aramaic.

With each new trip, I hope that I will finally see what comes next for me in this life. I'm always disappointed, but my Spirit Guide just laughs, so at least one of us is happy!

On one visit, a short, bald young man about twenty years old stood in a long robe, ten feet to my left. He was deeply engrossed in one of the books. I recognized him immediately as Grandpa Stefaniak, my dad's father, who died when I was three or four, so I didn't "recognize" him.

"Grandpa. It's me, Paulie. Al's son." I said excitedly. He never liked the name Paul and insisted on calling me Johnny. I remember the thrill of sneaking onto his throne-like chair in the living room when he wasn't around. He always chased me away but would eventually let me sit on his lap. He finally looked up; confused, at me and my two Angel escorts, and offered a simple nod and "Hey."

In an instant, I was whisked away by my Angels to another location before I could say anything. I couldn't explain how I knew it was my grandfather, but I did, and he was, without a doubt. He must have been nearly eighty when I was born, and I don't recall ever seeing any photos of him as a young man. I believe that my soul, or Higher Self, recognized him, and I must have been in the "Stefaniak Section" of The Akashic Records.

That's how this works. Once you access your soul or Higher Self, you are able to release a lifetime, or lifetimes, of information.

Animals

I have no doubt that in the past twenty-five years our cats, Mac, Mitts, Mabel, and Millie, have been able to see and interact with Angels and Spirit Guides in our homes.

In both Denver homes, I often saw Mac and Mitts sit upright on the family room sofa and lean into an unseen hand stroking them from head to tail. I could even see their fur being pressed down by these strokes. If you've spent time around cats, you understand how expressive they are when being petted. On many occasions I've seen all four cats sit and "box"—right and left jabs—as well as run and hide behind me, roll, jump, play, and chase with unseen friends.

When I meditated, our cats often came around, attracted by the energy. Once while I was meditating in our living room, Mitts jumped onto the ottoman that sat in the middle of a grouping of four chairs. Facing me, she stared and waited. When I asked her if she saw any-one in the room with us, she immediately turned to her left, still sitting stiffly upright, and stared at the empty chair on my right. She slowly bowed her head and then turned and bowed to the chair across from me, and then to the chair on my left. Finally, she turned back to face me with an "Anything else?" expression on her calm, little face. I believe she saw, or sensed, three Spirits sitting with me.

During another meditation in the living room, I opened my eyes a bit and saw a smiling man in his seventies with thinning white hair and a kind face. He was sitting in the chair to my right, just a few feet away. He wore a white robe with a braided, gold rope as a belt. He nodded "hello" and telepathically said that his name was Charles Orloff, a name unknown to me. Then he smiled, nodded, and disappeared.

After Mac and Mitts both passed away after eighteen good years as loving family members, I saw each of them in Spirit walking across the family room. Mitts was twenty feet away, as I sat in my easy chair. I looked up from my newspaper and saw her walk slowly past the television set and just disappear from right to left, head to tail, as if she passed into another dimension right before my eyes.

One year later, I sat reading on the family room sofa, and over the top of my book, I spotted Mac walk slowly past my feet, coming from my left to my right, before she also vanished into thin air just as Mitts had. In both cases, I was grateful to see them again and believed it was a gift to let me know that they were both safe on The Other Side.

Appliances & Electronics

Spirits can sometimes get your attention by focusing their energy on household items—turning them on or off, increasing or decreasing the volume or temperature, and the like.

Over the years I've found that, when I ask if Spirit is with me or when I'm about to meditate, appliances begin to make noise. Lamps or light fixtures begin to snap, crackle, or pop, or turn on and off. Televisions change channels when the remote control is out of everyone's reach. Volume goes up and down, or the TV turns itself on or off. This often happens when I'm speaking of my experiences to my wife, sons, or the few friends who know of them. I call them little "hellos," and I always follow up with an immediate request for the Spirits to reveal themselves. As I typed this paragraph, my head suddenly looked up from the keyboard, and my gaze fixed upon a small digital clock that read 3:36. That means nothing to you, but growing up I lived at 336 Weimar St., and before I began this writing session, I asked that the Angels and Guides on my "Team" to come and help. Now, my mother, father, and stepfather, all in Spirit, lived at 336 Weimar. Does that mean that they made me suddenly glance up from the keyboard to see 3:36 on the clock on the bookshelf as a way of letting me know they are here with me? Or is it just a coincidence?

I have over twenty years of head-turning and fixed-gaze experiences to believe that the Other Side tries to get my attention and make me aware of their presence. I found this message from my Angels in my notes: *Our presence makes your lamp pop because of the energy surrounding us.* I knew it!

I was on the phone with Cousin Eleanor years after her mom's passing. She mentioned that she sometimes felt her mom's presence, particularly while on the beach. As we chatted, our hallway smoke detector began to beep. It dawned on me that these beeps weren't random, but happened whenever one of us mentioned Eleanor's mom, Aunt Fran. That led us to a series of questions and answers: One beep meant "yes" and two meant "no." We were able to carry on an amazing little question-and-answer session with Aunt Fran in Heaven.

Aunt Fran invaded one of my meditations years later. I was visiting with Terry's parents and brother, when a very young Aunt Fran ran up, placed her hands on the shoulders of Bob and Brian and jumped up and over them. She was very excited, and she told me that her husband, Jay, would be joining her in Heaven by the first of the month.

And he did, passing over just a few days later. Aunt Fran knew about Uncle Jay's upcoming return Home and told me by interrupting a meditation visit, just as Bob had done the day before the passing of his wife, Ruby.

A final thought on appliances. In 1999, when we moved to Grand Junction, our family room had exposed speaker wires on both ends of a twelve-foot-high wall. I had a hard time with the small speakers. Each time I hung them, the wires would separate from the connectors. Every stinking time. One day I just asked my Angels for help. "I give up. Just make it work." Then ever so gently I hung both small speakers and prayed that the wires would stay connected. And they worked. Thirty days later I had an urge to check the wires, so I got the ladder and climbed up to one of the speakers, carefully peeking around the back of it. The sound from the *M*A*S*H* rerun on TV came out of the speaker perfectly, so what was I expecting to find anyway? Disconnected wires?

You got it. The wires hung loose from the wall and were not connected to the working speaker. I started to laugh, and then I moved the ladder to check the other speaker. It wasn't connected either. Two speakers worked perfectly for a month, and neither was connected to the wires in the wall.

I asked my Angels to take care of it, and they did. You can't make this stuff up.

As I prepared for a recent meditation, I asked for a physical sign that my Angels and Guides were with me. The reading lamp next to my chair began to crackle—it was off at the time—so what's crackling? Then the MP3 player resting on the notebook on my lap "jumped" to the floor in front of my feet. I bent over to pick it up and noticed that the power was now on, and my meditation tape was queued up and ready to play even though earlier I had been listening to a Simon & Garfunkel CD on my morning walk.

I took it to mean, *"We're here. Let's get started."* Fine with me. We did and had a wonderful session.

Books

Whenever I begin research for a screenplay or look for books on spirituality, I often ask Spirit what books I need to read and usually receive a message to visit a specific store where my Angels and Guides direct me to find important information.

Over the years books have flown off shelves and hit me in the head or torso, and the book would be exactly the one I needed to see. One of my happiest bookstore moments occurred one morning in a Barnes & Noble store, when a book flew off the bottom shelf and struck me in my foot instead of my head.

Another method they use is to grab my head, swivel it, and direct my gaze to a specific book. Retrieving it, I would find inevitably the book is just what I need. I clearly remember this happening twice while shopping for *Hello From Heaven!* by Bill Guggenheim and Judy Guggenheim, who address after-death communication. After I read their wonderful book, I wrote a letter sharing some of my after-death communications, and Judy called to discuss them and encouraged me to write my own book.

Thanks to Spirit, I have the perfect gift for friends who are grieving for recently Departed Loved Ones, as this paperback is often improperly shelved or overwhelmed by much larger books next to it. I quickly turn, hoping to catch a glimpse of my Angels or Guides as they swivel my poor head, but sadly, I never have.

The same thing happened to me after a telephone reading by gifted Houston psychic medium, Kim O'Neill. I read Kim's book, *How To Talk With Your Angels,* and I've had many readings from her over the phone. During one of them, she mentioned a Spirit Guide named King Vidor–a very unusual name–who was in a group of Guides working with me on a screenplay project. We both laughed that we were not familiar with this particular King, and wondered if he was an obscure biblical figure?

Well, Spirit made sure I'd get familiar. On my next bookstore visit, I suddenly stopped as my head was being turned hard and to the left towards shelves of leather-bound books. I was immediately drawn to one and opened it, ignoring the title. On the page before me, in bold print, was the name *King Vidor.* The book was about "Old Hollywood" and I learned that King Vidor was a distinguished director from Texas. As I typed "from Texas" in that last sentence, a voice in my head told me to add "distinguished," so I did. That's how this works. Before I started today's session I asked my Angels and Guides to come in and help me remember my experiences, and help with the writing.

About a year after the King Vidor book incident I was channel surfing and paused for no particular reason as a genial old man told a story of filmmaking. I hit the information button on the remote and learned that it was an *A&E* interview with KING VIDOR! I had to be "nudged" by Spirit to pause and listen because ESPN, a favorite, was on the next channel.

King Vidor has appeared in my meditations several times over the years. When I visit with a group of Guides in a conference room and learn their ideas on my current project, King joins in as a skinny young man in his twenties wearing an oversized cowboy hat. As I say my hellos, I always try to pull his hat down over his head for a laugh as he fends me off.

My Guides will "download" their ideas to me while I sleep - three a.m. always seems good for them - or type, but it's easier for me to meditate and take notes, and much easier than being hit in the head with a flying book.

Butterflies

Years after my Mother's death, I was back home in Buffalo, New York, visiting family. On my last day, I met my sister for breakfast, and afterwards, as we said our goodbyes in the restaurant's parking lot, we reminisced about Mom.

We stood between our cars. I had left my driver's side door wide open, and we heard a repeated "thump" nearby. I finally discovered the source. Inside my rental car, an exceptionally large black-and-orange butterfly kept flying into the window. I laughed and said that since we were talking about Mom, she sent a butterfly to say hello from her. Mom's house was filled with butterfly knick-knacks and wall art, so why wouldn't she send an oversized butterfly to grab our attention as we spoke of her? I lowered the window and freed the butterfly, and it floated around us for a bit as if saying goodbye before she flew away. "Bye, Mom." I said as I smiled and waved. I felt good thinking that she may have been there with us as we spoke of her.

Children and Angels

Everyone's heard a story about children playing with an imaginary friend, but what if they aren't imaginary? What if they were actually Angels or Spirit Guides who reveal themselves to children? Isn't that possible? Isn't that believable?

Perhaps they keep our children company, watch over them, and keep them from harm's way.

A friend's three-year-old son used to run around the house pretending, to throw, catch, and swing a bat. When his parents asked what he was doing, he'd matter-of-factly reply "I'm playing baseball with the Angels," and then he'd be off again-running and playing.

The first time I met this boy's two-month-old brother, he was so excited to see me-kicking his legs and waving his hands as if his soul recognized me. We went to the kitchen table, and the baby was on the family room sofa surrounded by a mountain of pillows. We could see and hear him as he carried on a running conversation with an invisible "someone" above him, and he was obviously enjoying every second of it.

I bumped-into a friend's sister several months after he passed away. We were in James Van Praagh's workshop at a conference in Arizona and I learned that another child had been born into this wonderful family. The mother could hear her daughter giggling and babbling from her crib over the monitor. When she checked on her, there would be no one there, but this baby would always walk over to a photo of the grandfather she never met and smother it with kisses. If she wasn't seeing and talking to Angels in her bedroom, I imagine she met her Grandpa in Spirit.

I met my ex-sister-in-law's twins for the only time when they were three-years-old. We brought a raggedy doll for the girl and a truck for the boy. I was sitting in the kitchen when they turned together and stared hard at me. I realized I could hear them telepathically, asking if I remembered them from their school with Michael when I visited with the Angel. Say what? Michael was their departed uncle who passed before they were born. During a meditation I was taken to a small grass hut with one of my Guardian Angels. We interrupted a class Michael was teaching to one dozen young children who sat on the floor before him. He was confused to see me, and my Angel explained my presence to him. He had died tragically and it was nice to see him happy and working with children.

I was so stunned to see Michael that I never noticed the faces of the children who turned around to look at me. I stared back at the twins and mentally told them that I had only focused on Michael, but I was happy they remembered me. It appears Michael spent time in Heaven with the twins before they were born to his sister. At the age of three, they still remembered their time with him and recognized me from my visit. The twins soon relaxed and the girl came over and sat on my lap, surprising their family. I never mentioned our "connection" to anyone.

Seeing an Angel with me makes Spirits in Heaven stop and take pause. They must realize that I don't belong there and since I'm always in the company of one or two Guardian Angels, my presence is a shock to them as well. I don't get the impression that the Spirits I'm allowed to see or those who are able to pop-in and say hello to me, are in the company of Angels much.

I recently saw Michael while meditating for only the second time in just over twenty years. Two Spirits, one male and one female, arrived as I was about to separate from the session. As they came into focus, I saw that it was Michael and his mother, Ann, who passed-over earlier that year. She looked very young and gave me a little smile and nod. Ann was a lovely lady and my former mother-in-law, and it was great to see her reunited with her son.

At the beginning of this section, I mentioned Angels protecting children from harm, and I have the story to prove it.

When my son, Chris, started walking at twelve months, escaping from his crib was his greatest joy. Minutes after he was tucked in each night, he would run down the hall and into the family room with open arms and a huge smile on his face. Then he would clap his hands and laugh. *"Ta-Da! Here I am. I'm not sleepy. Let's play some more!"* That's what he seemed to say.

One night I snuck back to see how this ingenious little fellow escaped from his crib. I stood outside his bedroom and peeked around the corner as he pulled himself up on the top of the crib railing, balanced atop it, and then swung his legs over. He hung by his hands and then dropped to the floor.

So cool! That didn't last long. Joel was born two months later, and Chris was banished to a new bedroom and a big-boy bed with no railings, but it had a new obstacle—a doorway fence.

One evening Chris sat at his drawing desk, as I watched television in the family room. Nature called, and I slipped away to the adjoining bathroom, not stopping to place the child's fence in the doorway. Shortly thereafter, I opened the door of the bathroom, stepped out into the corridor, and witnessed a sight I will never forget.

Chris hovered in the air over the third step of our steep staircase and about three feet above the floor level. Wearing only a diaper, he waved his arms and legs and giggled. I took a step-and-a-half and lunged forward, grabbing the edge of a wall with my left hand for balance.

I reached out with my right hand, slid my fingers inside the top of his diaper, and yanked him back to my chest. I hugged him tightly and stepped away from the landing. I was out of breath and in shock. Chris giggled with delight. We went back into the family room, and I quickly put the fence back into place and never again failed to do so.

I believe an Angel saved Chris' life that night. An Angel caught him as he started to fall down the stairs and held him in place until I arrived. Chris wasn't falling; he was hovering three feet up and out. One-year-olds don't hover in the air by design or by accident. An Angel must have saved him from a tragic fall. Angels are sent by God to guard us, from birth until death, and hopefully protect us from our stupid mistakes and accidents.

Dream Weaving

I usually have pretty dull dreams—nothing extraordinary, just *extra ordinary*. Some where I'm back in high school and warming up for a basketball or baseball game, but I never get to play because I awaken. Another recurring high school dream involves being told I can't graduate because I haven't turned in some assignment, and I say that it doesn't matter because I already graduated from the University of Colorado and I also have an MBA, so I ignore the exam and wake up.

Many times over the years I've noticed a Departed Loved One standing in the middle of the action. They aren't a part of the dream but simply a part of the background. They smile and wave, catching my attention. "Hey, that's my mom," I say to myself and the dream continues.

What I believe is really happening is that I Astral Travel and go someplace where I meet up with other Spirits who escape while asleep and return to the Other Side where we discuss our present lives. It seems like therapy because I often remember complaining about "the life I chose" and "what the heck was I thinking about when I did?" Seeing departed family members and friends is always a treat for me, but they've been showing up in my meditations for over twenty years, and, while brief, these are better "quality time," when we can have brief conversations.

I recall one very vivid dream in the mid-1990s, when I awakened from a Saturday afternoon nap with a start, excited and in a cold sweat and clutching my right shoulder, as my wife and son walked into the house from a shopping trip. I was dreaming that I was a young frontiersman trapped on a raft with a handful of other men, and we were floating slowly down a river. Using crates for cover, we fired our muskets at Native Americans who ran along the shore shooting arrows at us. I fired a shot and before I could duck back down, an arrow struck me in the shoulder, and I awoke.

I still have continuous pain in that shoulder and never had rotator cuff surgery on it because of the ugly scars it left. Two chiropractors, working on my right shoulder, screamed and jumped back when their fingertips slipped into the tear. I wonder if my injury was new or left over as a reminder from a previous incarnation as a frontiersman.

Who's There?

Knocking on wood is Spirit's way of letting you know that they are here. Occasionally, when I lie in bed at night and ask my Angels for guidance and healing while I sleep, my words are met with loud knocks or cracks, like thunder hitting the floor, ceiling, and walls. The power of these sounds would make you think our house was falling apart, but thankfully, it's not.

In our Denver home, I remember asking if anyone was with me as I was about to drift off one night in bed, and a loud pounding on the wall two feet above my head came a second later, scaring the bejeezus out of me. I saw psychic medium Sylvia Brown on a television show, and she answered a question from the audience about knocks. She said that they were Spirits, not the sound of your house settling because how many years does it take for a house to settle?

My thoughts precisely.

Play That Tune

Spirits seem to have the ability either to tap into musical energy and manipulate it or tap into my consciousness and make me think of a certain person, place, or thing to match a song that is about to be played.

For example, during the month of December, I usually play Christmas music exclusively in the home and car. The rest of the year, if I ask if my Angels are around, I get bombarded with Christmas music or any song with "Angel" in the title or lyrics. These aren't songs that I would normally think of, and they just pop into my head.

Very often when I drive in the car with my wife and tell her "the same stories," songs that are relevant to my story come on the radio. In the late 1970s, a friend from Florida came to visit with his wife. As we took day trips around the state, he would nap in the back seat, then "awaken" to sing along with James Taylor's "Julie" in a funny falsetto. This friend passed away thirty years ago, but whenever I talk about him, "Julie" plays on the car radio. So, are Angels playing that song, or is my friend, in Spirit, tuning the radio? Or am I being influenced to talk about him because that song is about to be played? Last month this friend made a surprise appearance during a meditation and said, *"Hello Son, God you got old."* Well, that's what thirty years will do to you. He always called me "Son," although he was only ten years older than me.

While writing a letter to someone about my spiritual experiences, I had the CD player set to play random songs. I asked my Angels and Spirits to play Harry Belafonte's "Mary's Boy Child" as a sign that they were present when I reached a specific event I was relating, and they did—a one-in-seventy-five chance or a 1.33 percent chance. Coincidence?

One morning I was talking to my wife about my latest meditation. I held the TV remote in my hand, and we heard a loud click come from the components, as the sound suddenly shifted from the television to DVD, as if ensuring Terry would be able to hear my message.

Recently I took a break from writing to check the mail. When I returned to the kitchen, I chuckled to myself and said aloud, "What will my sons think of me when they read this book?"

In my head I immediately heard Chris's voice saying, "My dad's messed up." The television was tuned to a '80s music channel, and I heard Joan Jett's "I Love Rock 'n Roll" from 1982 playing in the background.

I used to sing that song to my sons, Chris and Joel, only I'd change the lyrics to "I Love Chris 'n Joel." They thought that was the coolest thing ever, since they were toddlers, and I sang over Joan so they could only hear their names.

My point is that, as I was thinking of their reactions, their "theme song" came on and made me notice. I laughed. It's just another little "hello" in my world.

The Right Number

Spirit sometimes uses a telephone as a direct means of communication to a loved one as many authors have written.

It happened to me in May 1991, five months after my mother passed away. When she was alive, she would call and leave a message in the same singsong voice every time—"Hi Paul, it's only Mom." After I dropped the boys off at baseball practice one afternoon, I returned home to find two new phone messages. The first was from my son's friend—"Chris. Pat. Call me." I've heard that one a million times over the years.

The second message gave me the chills. "Hi, Paul, it's only Mom." Five months after she died? This was back when we had a tape-recorded message machine, and phone messages were received and erased daily. After five months of phone messages for our family being erased daily, what is the possibility that a message from Mom survived that long? What are the odds? Let's say there were 150 days of phone messages received and erased on that tape, and then an "old message" from the beginning of the tape—the second message in—survived five months. I don't think so. I was spooked and immediately called my sister. Her husband told me not to tell her because she wouldn't deal with it well. And I never have.

A few days later, during a meditation—probably my third month of it—my Mom came through to me for the first time, bursting onto the scene as her face emerged from a billowy white cloud, seemingly a few feet above me.

"You did it! You did it! It's me. You made contact, it's me!" I was shocked. The connection was broken immediately, and the meditation ended. I believe that she did come through via the phone call to encourage me to continue meditating.

That was the first of over two hundred visits from Mom during my meditations. I'll never forget it or hearing her voice on the answering machine.

Psychometry

Psychometry occurs when you hold someone's personal object, sense the energy that has been absorbed, and receive messages through a touch from Spirit.

About seven hundred people attended a workshop in Denver with psychic medium James Van Praagh, and he had us pair off. I sat knee-to-knee with a pleasant, blonde woman from New Mexico. She held my house key in her hand, closed her eyes, and rubbed it gently between her fingers. She described seeing a little dog and a boat, and I had absolutely no idea what she was talking about.

Two days later while I was driving home through the mountains, I remembered that the previous owners of our home had a little dog and a small boat. They parked it in a space next to the garage, and the husband used to take the dog fishing with him. Their energies, not mine, were still imprinted on the house key two years later. I look for this woman at spiritual events, hoping to correct my mistake. After I ruined her psychometry experience, I took my turn. She handed me a woman's ring. I closed my eyes and turned it over and over in my hands.

A young woman in Spirit came through, appearing an arm's length away near my partner's right shoulder. She had straight, blonde hair parted in the middle and wore a pale blue sleeveless dress with small flowers—gold petals with a maroon center. She was very intense and glared at me as she telepathically spoke to me. Her message was very personal, and I don't recall the details, only that my partner sobbed, and I wanted to get away from this scowling Spirit but couldn't. I had to finish relaying her message.

My partner said the young woman I described was unfamiliar and not her daughter. Her daughter had been a bartender in Albuquerque and was murdered. She went to that bar on her daughter's next birthday, and glasses flew off the shelves and shattered.

The emotion of this experience was extremely unpleasant for me. I felt trapped between the Spirit's intense energy and my partner's tears. I was successful in contacting a Spirit, but my message was nothing but bad news.

In 2011 in Phoenix at a session with psychic medium and nice guy, John Holland, I attempted another psychometry demonstration. I was paired with a quiet Hispanic woman, who gave me an ornate, antique-looking ladies watch to hold. In a few seconds I asked if her parents had given it as a gift for her thirty-sixth birthday.

"No. I gave it to myself for my thirty-sixth birthday."

Sorry, but I got "thirty-sixth" and "birthday gift" correct.

Suddenly, a "screen" appeared behind her left shoulder. I saw two young Hispanic women who could be twins standing shoulder-to-shoulder as they held hands and giggled. They wore flowery summer dresses with their hair in buns but loose on the sides. It may have been the 1940s or 1950s, and they were standing in a backyard in Texas that seemed to go on forever.

I kept hearing "Two Grandmas" over and over in my head, but my partner wasn't buying it. She wanted to hear from her departed mother, not her grandmothers. This was bad. I have an unimpressed partner, disappointed at what I'm telling her, and two giggling Spirits who would rather talk to themselves than me. I asked a few times if her grandmother was a twin, and waited for her answer. "No. But she had a sister who looked just like her. And I called her Grandma, too."

Grandma too? Thank you! Two Grandmas! Hello?

The Two Grandmas proceeded to thank her for coming and encouraged her to continue her spiritual endeavors. My partner was not pleased at all. She wanted to hear from her mother and wouldn't be satisfied with anyone else.

Her mother came through the next day in a workshop with the English psychic medium, Lisa Williams, and it was an amazing visit. This mother and my partner had some serious unresolved issues, and their closure was witnessed by the two hundred attendees. It seemed that her mother needed a gifted professional medium to help with this reunion, not an amateur like me.

I've always been good with Grandmas, though.

Do You Smell That?

Spirit is able to provide smells that are associated with Departed Loved Ones. No possible physical source is present, but you are absolutely certain that it is real. If you are like me, you search for the source like a person possessed.

When I first became interested in Spiritual topics and my own development, I attended a two-day seminar put on by a national speaker's association. I remember guest speaker after guest speaker telling the same story about a boy throwing a beached starfish back into the water and his father saying that there are so many starfish on the sand that it didn't matter. The punch line was *"It matters to that one,"* which makes it a cute story with a moral.

I later wrote to the association's president, a delightful woman, and shared some of my spiritual experiences. I wondered if, in the mid-1990s, there would be any market for speakers discussing spiritual topics.

As I wrote the letter and described how I visited my grandmother's Arrival Party, I suddenly smelled my grandmother's breaded pork chops—the amazing ones that she made in a monstrous black pan whenever her family got together. The savory aroma of her iconic dish was wafting through the house and up to the office loft.

It can't be, I thought, as I raced downstairs to the kitchen. I threw open the oven door, and it was empty. There were no pork chops on the counters or in the fridge. It was a little "hello" from Grandma in Heaven. She knew that I was thinking of her. I did get a reply weeks later from Madam President. She didn't believe there would be a market for anyone discussing spirituality and suggested—ever so politely— that Duke University had a program for people with my mental issues and I should look into it.

Hey, Read This!

When Spirit wants to send us a message, our attention is drawn to signs, billboards, and other printed things to make the point. I once had trouble getting a specific problem out of my mind. "Ruminating" on it would be kind to say, but "obsessed" would be far more accurate. I was reliving and reviewing this issue as I got out of my car in a restaurant parking lot. My head was suddenly turned hard to the left and down towards the bumper sticker on a nearby car. It read: "Get Over It!"

Fine, fine—just don't break my neck.

A week after my heart attack in 2000, we attended a going-away party for Terry's boss. There was a large sheet cake with a lengthy message written on the icing. Pieces were cut from all four sides, and at the end of the evening the cake looked like one hot mess. A woman decided to cut the remainder of the cake into small pieces for folks to take home. I happened to pass by, glanced at the cake, and grabbed her wrist before she made the first cut. I called Terry's boss and his wife over to the table.

"Look, there's a message from your Angels," I said, pointing to the four haphazard words, the only ones that remained on the cake:

God Bless Good Ken

They took photos of the message to show their family, and in the moment, we laughed and agreed that it indeed was a message from his Angels. After the party, I carried the cake to their car. As we all walked through the parking lot, I kept hearing, *"Tell them, tell them it was us—their Angels. Tell them."*

I casually looked around, but my anxious eyes saw no Angels nearby. Of course, I didn't mention the shouting because I didn't want anyone to think I was crazy, probably like the millions of other Americans who keep these experiences to themselves.

Hey! Check Me Out

A visage is what we look like on the Other Side. Rather than some ghostly apparition, this is an Earth-like representation of how we choose to appear. We can make any changes that we'd like. Is your mind racing yet? Are you visualizing the new and improved you yet? Go ahead.

Our souls recognize other souls by their energies, so appearance is irrelevant. Don't worry, be happy. Be healthy, young, and beautiful or handsome again. When meditating, my departed family and friends appear, and I qualify every visit. I cannot be thinking of an individual or begin the meditation by hoping someone specific comes through. That would be influencing my subconscious, so they must "pop in uninvited," or else I dismiss their visit.

Sometimes individuals appear, looking different than I remember them, and sometimes I never met them before. Puzzled, I will tell my Angels, "I have no idea who this person is." In an instant, a photograph or a memory of that person will flash before me. This has happened with Terry's father, Bob, her Aunt Fran, a family friend, and my best friend's parents, plus his "Grammy."

I remember an encounter from 1991, when I began my spiritual journey, with what I believe was my Heavenly visage or Higher Self. As I walked into our master bathroom, the reflection in the mirror immediately caught my attention, mostly because it wasn't mine!

The Man in the Mirror was a handsome, smiling, deeply-tanned fellow in his thirties. He had silver, perfectly-styled hair, wore aviator glasses, and dressed in a white polo shirt and white shorts. He looked like a tennis pro. He was also at least a head shorter than me. I'm six-foot-five and had short, dark hair at that time.

Amazed, I froze and stared. He smiled and laughed, and I dashed out. I avoided that room for days, and even then I'd peek around the corner at the mirror before I would commit to entering fully.

Looking back, I really liked his look and wouldn't mind one tiny bit if this handsome fellow were my Higher Self, giving me a preview of my visage once I return to Heaven. Think of it—the best possible you at your best age—and without any surgery, dieting, hair procedures, or expense.

Go on, take a moment while the classic lyrics, "Heaven, I'm in Heaven..." play in your head. It's fun.

With my luck, it was probably my playful Spirit Guide, Dan, messing with me again by getting my hopes up for a chance at eternal handsomeness.

As you read this chapter, did you note all of the "little stuff" that you also may have experienced but dismissed because you didn't connect it to Spirit communication? These experiences range from simple actions of animals and butterflies to vivid visits by loved ones in dreams, to unaccountable noises and messages via songs and signs, or as complex as a child's "imaginary friend"—or in my son's case a "lifesaving invisible friend."

Are you now more willing to entertain the possibility that Spirit has, or is, attempting to capture your attention, and are willing to do whatever is necessary to make their presence known?

It happened to me, and it could happen to you—if it hasn't already.

But only if you are open to it, only if you remain present and accepting because...

We are all connected to Heaven.

twenty-seven
What Have I Learned?

I am sensitive to Spirit in all of its forms: Ghosts, Angels, Guides, and Departed Loved Ones.

My soul or Spirit will come forward and make me aware of what I need to know, and whom I need to meet or avoid.

Spirit uses us as they wish—to keep us on our paths or help us when we, or others, are in need.

We can talk to God or Spirit and get an immediate response. When I was about to die, I realized that I wasn't ready or given a choice. My cries were answered, and my life saved by two miracles.

Deathbed visitations are real. They are joyful, and the promise of Heaven and an afterlife are revealed to us.

Once we open ourselves to Spirit, we are able to connect and receive ongoing contact, guidance, and information.

We all have Spirit Guides who watch over us and work with us in various facets of our lives, which are all about growing spiritually to honor God.

Accessing our past lives through regressions is amazing, and we "know" that the scenes, emotions, and events are real.

We are all able to see, hear, feel, and know Spirit communication once we accept the fact and look for it.

In times of danger or possible Exit Points, Spirit can make themselves known and provide assistance.

Spirit communicates through love, warmth, compassion, and humor. Our Loved Ones are happy, healthy, and thrilled to connect with us once again.

Seeing Spirit is a remarkable, unforgettable experience that is truly a gift from God.

At conferences and workshops, like-minded people on spiritual journeys of their own provide a welcoming and supportive environment where overwhelming spiritual energy can provide unimaginable experiences.

We choose the lessons we are here to learn, and Spirit works to keep us on path but will not impose guidance and assistance upon our Free Will.

When you ask Spirit for a sign of their presence—be prepared, be aware, and be amazed.

Acknowledge Spirit's role, help, and presence in your life. Give thanks.

We are loved unconditionally. Death is merely a transition from this life to one in Heaven. Here, I am not my clothing. I am my mind and body. When I leave this life, I am no longer my mind and body, I am my Soul. I am Spirit. I am in Heaven. I am Immortal.

I no longer fear death other than being separated from my family, but know that I will be reunited with them in Heaven.

You don't have to believe in Heaven or life-after-death while alive. My departed family members have come through with the same message—they had no idea this was possible—yet once you pass over and become the Guest of Honor at your own Arrival Party, all doubt will vanish. As my grandmother said...

"Hey, this(Heaven)ain't so bad."

Indeed.

And Amen.

Conclusion

"Don't be defensive about your life. Very few can do what you do. Very few have been selected to do the work you will do. We will be there to help with your memory. You'll see. Be grateful and happy that this time has arrived."

This is all a gift given to me by God, I believe, and I humbly treat it as such. When drowning and about to die, I asked, "Is that all You wanted from me?"—and my life was saved by His Miracle. Everything since then has been, as Arianna always reminds me, *"In God's Hands, In God's Time."* I can see what I'm shown, and hear what I'm allowed to, with my fullest understanding that I do this by God's Grace and not my own ability.

I am still striving to fulfill my destiny; to fulfill the promise that I made while pleading for my life; to do the work I have been shown by my Angels and Guides. I have been instructed to record my spiritual experiences—my own journey—for my wife and sons, and perhaps for the public at large.

It's time to check where you are on your own ladder. Did you climb higher as you read, eager to seek out more information and recall experiences of your own? Here's the secret: Your ladder will keep rising, and rungs will be added because you will continue to search, learn, and grow until you return Home. Maybe you stayed safely in place, certain this isn't for you.

Some of us have undoubtedly begun our spiritual journeys. Others are becoming aware and inspired to begin theirs. Relevant books, workshops and conferences, similarly-minded folks, and meditation are there to help you experience what is already within you. Meditate and be open to the experience, and then see what happens. Ask God for help and then listen and trust what you hear. You can light a candle or live in the darkness—the choice is always yours. Imagine making contact with a Departed Loved One and truly know that they are happy in Heaven, and aware of what is happening in your life? What would it mean to you to experience Angels and Guides in your life, and see that they are patiently waiting for you to connect with them?

Thank you for reading this book. I'll close by sharing a lovely parting message my Angels say to me. It always caresses my heart and soul, and I hope you feel it as well.

"Go in God's Peace and Love...
until the day you come Home
to God's Peace and Love."

Made in the USA
Lexington, KY
23 May 2016